# THE PRACTICE OF CONJOINT
# THERAPY

*Psychotherapy Series*

**The Initial Interview in Psychotherapy**
Argelander, H., M.D.

**Children and Their Parents in Brief Therapy**
Barten, H. H., M.D., Barten, S. S., Ph.D. (eds.)

**Brief Therapies**
Barten, H., M.D. (ed.)

**The Art of Empathy**
Bullmer, K., Ed.D.

**Basic Psychological Therapies**
Fix, A. J., Ph.D. and Haffke, E. A., M.D.

**Assert Yourself!**
Galassi, M.D., Ed.D. and Galassi, J. P., Ph.D.

**The Group as Agent of Change**
Jacobs, A., Ph.D. and Spradlin, W., M.D. (eds.)

**Psychodrama**
Greenberg, I. A., Ph.D. (ed.)

**The Narcissistic Condition**
Nelson, M. C. (ed.)

**Emotional Flooding**
Olsen, P. T., Ph.D.

**The Couch**
Stern, H., Ph.D.

**Psychotherapy and the Role of the Environment**
Voth, H. M., M.D. and Orth, M. H., M.S.W.

**The Therapeutic Self**
Watkins, J. G., Ph.D.

**Clinical Child Psychology**
Williams, G. J., Ph.D. and Gordon, S., Ph.D. (eds.)

**Family Therapy**
Zuk, G. H., Ph.D.

**The Practice of Conjoint Therapy**
Ormont, L. R., Ph.D.

# The Practice of Conjoint Therapy
## *Combining Individual and Group Treatment*

**Louis R. Ormont, Ph.D.**
*Clinical Professor, Adelphi University, New York*
**Herbert S. Strean, D.S.W.**
*Distinguished Professor, Rutgers University, New Jersey*

**HUMAN SCIENCES PRESS**
72 Fifth Avenue    3 Henrietta Street
NEW YORK, NY 10011 ● LONDON, WC2E 8LU

Library of Congress Catalog Number 77–17079

ISBN: 0-87705-335-3

Copyright © 1978 by Human Sciences Press
72 Fifth Avenue, New York, New York 10011

Printed in the United States of America
89 987654321

**Library of Congress Cataloging in Publication Data**

Ormont, Louis R
    The practice of conjoint therapy.

    Bibliography: p.
    1. Psychotherapy.  2. Group psychotherapy.
I. Strean, Herbert S., joint author.  II. Title.
RC480.5.075    616.8'915    77-17079
ISBN 0-87705-335-3

# CONTENTS

# PREFACE

The past decade has witnessed the introduction and popularization of many therapeutic modalities: family therapy, crisis intervention, encounter and sensitivity groups, marathons, and a host of others. Practitioners and theorists of psychotherapy, social work, and psychoanalysis are increasingly recognizing that treatment, to be effective, must adapt to the patient's unique maturational needs and life story, characterological armor, distinctive defenses, and familial and social circumstances. In lieu of requiring the patient to conform to a preconceived therapeutic model, practitioners are more frequently taking the position that the treatment modality, therapeutic atmosphere, and transference relationship with the therapist must be tailored to the patient and his ego strengths and limitations, fixations, quality of object relatedness, frustration tolerance, and other psychosocial dimensions.

This book is an attempt to explicate how one form of treatment, conjoint therapy, has been effective for hundreds of patients who have concomitantly participated in two forms of therapy with two different therapists, i.e., individual psychotherapy and group therapy. The book will demonstrate through case vignettes and with pertinent theoretical underpinning how many troubled individuals can strengthen their ego functions; relate to others with more autonomy and gratification; enhance their self-image, self-esteem, and identity; and discard neurotic and other disabling and self-defeating behavior and attitudes by concomitantly being treated in individual and group treatment.

As will be demonstrated in the text, the authors, who have practiced conjoint treatment for close to two decades, are wedded to a psychosocial view of the human being which makes "conjoint treatment" an inevitable corollary. Almost from birth the individual human organism has to attempt two crucial tasks: coping, interacting, and transacting with others and coping, interacting, and transacting with himself. These two psychosocial requirements are, of course, mutually interdependent. The child's self-esteem, body image, reality testing, etc. will affect his perceptions of and interactions with others; furthermore, his interactions with significant others will influence his self-image and other ego functions.

Conjoint treatment takes into consideration the aforementioned facets of human functioning. As the patient studies his fantasies, dreams, fears, and transference reactions in his individual therapy, he can experiment in the group setting and learn how his strengths and limitations are perceived and received by others. As he discovers in the group setting some of his characteristic means of handling interpersonal relations and interpersonal conflicts, particularly the anxiety that is involved therein, he can then go on to examine more microscopically in individual therapy some of the historical antecedents and other aspects of his dysfunctional interpersonal behavior.

Conjoint treatment provides a paradigm of the world, an opportunity for the patient to examine and experience himself within a one-to-one intimate relationship, with two parental figures, as well as within the world of the group. All of these experiences dynamically affect and enrich each other.

In sum, the purpose of this book is to present the therapeutic rationale of conjoint therapy, how it is linked to a psychosocial understanding of the human being, and through clinical vignettes, demonstrate the mechanics and dynamics of conjoint therapy. The clinical examples together with metapsychological explanations and interpretations will demonstrate for the reader how this form of therapy can uniquely enhance therapeutic growth and psychosocial functioning.

*Chapter 1*

# TOWARDS A PSYCHOLOGICAL VIEW OF THE HUMAN BEING

Any sound approach to psychotherapy should rest on a coherent and internally consistent orientation to the human being. In this chapter, we will attempt to explicate how we view human functioning both in its adaptive and pathological forms. As we have studied our patients over the past two decades, we have been very much influenced by Freud's metapsychological view of the human organism. Enriching our orientation are the formulations of theorists such as Hartmann, Erikson, Anna Freud, and others, whose contributions we shall also briefly review.

## FREUD'S METAPSYCHOLOGICAL APPROACH

In contrast to many static notions about the human being existing in the late 1800s, Sigmund Freud postulated the principle of *psychic determinism.* This principle holds that in mental functioning, nothing happens by chance. Each psychic event, whether it be the appearance of a neurotic symptom, a dream, or a temper tantrum, is determined by the ones that preceded it.[9, 11] Freudian psychoanalysis has constantly assumed that everything human is meaningful— a slip of the tongue, coming late for an appointment, a sleepless or restful night, etc. Man is seen as an organism who is driven by unconscious, instinctually derived forces, which exert more power over his behavior than his alleged reason. These forces, according to the Freudian theorist and therapist, can be brought to consciousness and eventually under the person's control.[9, 25]

Freud posited another basic and related principle, namely, that consciousness is an exceptional rather than a regular attribute of psychic processes. He said, "It is precisely the fact that so much of what goes on in our minds is unconscious, that is, unknown to ourselves, that accounts for the apparent discontinuities in our mental lives."[11] In addition, Freud contended that no behavior can be seen in isolation from the total personality: "all behavior is integral to, and characteristic of the behaving personality."[11]

In Freud's view, the human personality can be seen from several distinct but intermeshing points of view, and it is these dimensions of psychic functioning that combine to make up what is known as the *metapsychological* approach to the human personality.

The *dynamic* dimension, or Freud's instinct theory, is concerned with the ultimate dynamics of personality functioning. Psychic energy, according to Freud, derives from a state of excitation in the body that has been created by somatic processes: "Instinct appears to us as a borderline concept between the mental and physical."[11] A drive releases tension which creates motor activity. After a cessation of tension, there is gratification. The direction implicit in this sequence is called the "pleasure principle" and helps us understand wishes, fantasies, dreams, and other phenomena.[9, 11] The pleasure principle connotes a dimension in man which seeks gratification—libidinal and aggressive discharge—and seeks to avoid pain. The amount of psychic energy which is directed toward another human being or object is known as *cathexis.*[20]

The *genetic* dimension posits that personality patterns are "functions of constitutional predispositions as shaped by previous experiences and present situational pressures."[11] Each individual's past in many ways determines his present. Consequently, the therapist is always interested in studying with his patient the story of his life in order to determine how it is being recapitulated in the present.[21, 23]

During the first five or six years of life the child experiences a series of dynamically differentiated stages that are of extreme importance for the formation of personality. During the oral stage, the mouth is the main focus of activity; it is not only the principal organ through which nourishment is provided but also offers the first experience in a relationship with another human being. If it is a successful experience, the child can learn to trust himself and others; if not, the depleting experiences attending this period can lead to disorders such as paranoia and possibly schizophrenia.[4]

In the second year of life, following the oral period, the child turns his interests to elimination functions. During the anal period, the child learns some autonomy and that he can say, "no." If limits are appropriately provided by the parents, the child gains a sense of autonomy. Otherwise he can emerge into a rather reckless, impulsive, dependent personality if limits and structure have not been appropriately provided; if, on the other hand, limits are premature or arbitrary, the individual can emerge as obsessive, compulsive, and rigid in his attitudes and behavior.

During the phallic phase the central complex is the oedipal, in which the child wishes to replace a parent of the same sex and to have sex or bodily contact with the parent

of the opposite sex.[9] Because the child often fears retaliation and/or loss of love from the parent of the same sex,
he gradually decathects the parent of the opposite sex and
moves into a period of instinctual quiescence.[25] As a result
of oedipal wishes, the boy is dominated by castration anxiety and the girl is dominated by penis envy. Reuben Fine
has pointed out that while Freud believed that penis envy
is biological, most authors today adhere to the conviction
that it is cultural. "In view of the attack levied upon this
concept by the Women's Liberation Movement," Fine
states, "it should be emphasized that penis envy is essentially a clinical observation about what women feel, not a
derogation of women."[9]

Puberty brings a recrudescence of the biological
drives, a revival of oedipal interests, and ambivalence towards parents and authority. It is during this period that
the adolescent begins to form his or her sexual identity and
other lifetime roles. At puberty a new sexual aim appears,
namely, the discharge of the sexual product; all the other
aims become subordinated to this one. A loved object must
be chosen towards which there is a combination of tender
and erotic impulses.[9] Adolescent love relationships, because they revive oedipal and incestuous interests are typi-
cally stormy and ambivalent.[4, 9]

The *topographic* model examines the personality in
terms of conscious, and unconscious states of mind. The
conscious is that part of our mental activities that we are
fully aware of at any time; the preconscious refers to
thoughts and feelings that can be brought into consciousness fairly easily, and the unconscious refers to thoughts,
feelings, desires, and memories of which we are not aware
but which influence all of our behavior. The unconscious
consists not only of drives, defenses, and admonitions but
contains the memories of events and attitudes that have
been repressed.[10, 11]

The primary process reigns in the unconscious. Its

chief characteristic is the striving for immediate discharge and the two major devices of the primary process are condensation and displacement. In condensation, one idea stands for many and in displacement, ideas or feelings are shifted from one area to another. A third device of primary process is symbolization, which allows for representation of unconscious material in conscious life because it conceals the true meaning of the detail.[9]

The *structural,* or tripartite, point of view refers to the psychic structure of id, ego, and superego. The id, the most primitive part of the mind and totally unconscious is the repository of the drives and is concerned with their gratification. The ego develops out of experience and reason, is the executive, mediates between the inner world of the drives, superego commands, and the demands of the external world. It judges, reasons, frustrates wishes and has other functions such as object relations or relations with other people. The ego erects defenses against anxiety. It is the functioning of the ego that helps us diagnose our patients' strengths and weaknesses, and as we observe in his adaptation which ego functions are working well and which are not, we can assess the severity of his disturbances. The more severe the patient's disturbances, the less operative are his ego functions and vice versa.[22, 23]

The superego is the judge or censor of our minds and is essentially the product of interpersonal experiences. Essentially, the superego is the internal representative of the parents which arises after the resolution of the oedipus complex at about five or six years of age.[12] The superego is the storehouse of our "do's and don'ts," values and imperatives.

The *economic* dimension of Freud's theory of personality holds that all behavior is regulated by, and its function is to dispose of psychological energy. Rappaport has pointed out that psychological energies "cannot be expressed in the mathematical formulae in which physics expresses its energy concepts, yet they are referents of phenomena which seem to abide by the laws of energy exchange—conservation, entropy, and least action." [20] The human psychic organism can be viewed as an open system in which psychological energies derived from drives are expressed, discharged, dammed up, stored or transformed into thought and action.[25]

## NEUROTIC SYMPTOMS AND OTHER MALADAPTATIONS: THE FREUDIAN VIEW

When the individual's sexual or aggressive drives or impulses are unacceptable to the ego, the ego utilizes defenses to protect the person against conscious awareness of ideas, thoughts, and memories that are unbearable. Defenses such as repression, projection, and denial help insulate the person from feeling anxiety. Anxiety, according to Freud, is a warning to the person that some unacceptable thought or action will reach consciousness.[26]

If the impulse is too strong or the defense too weak, anxiety erupts and the person forms a neurotic symptom. The symptom such an obsession or a phobia expresses simultaneously the individual's id impulse and his dread of the impulse. In a phobia, for example, two variables are operative: the very situation that the individual fears also excites him—aggressive people or situations, sexual scenes or seductive people, etc. Within a Freudian orientation neuroses are "arranged" by the person to effect a compromise between id impulses and those parts of the personality which repudiate the expression of sexual and/or aggressive impulses.

Many individuals entering psychotherapy may manifest character defects or "character disorders." Here, there are no neurotic symptoms but the conflict expresses itself in character traits such as obstinacy, extreme dependency, Don Juanism, etc. Anxiety in these "ego syntonic" activities is not aroused but the individual's character defects inevitably bring him into conflict in his interpersonal relationships.

For both neurotics and those with character disorders, the individual has regressed or is fixated at childish levels of development and is trying to gratify immature fantasies and wishes but concomitantly is defending against them. When the ego is very fragile and many of its functions are not working well, id impulses and superego admonitions that are usually defended against in the more mature person emerge, and we have a psychosis.

Finally, in psychosomatic problems the anxiety that erupts is converted into somatic expression and the individual then manifests symptoms like ulcers, migraine headaches, heart palpitations, etc.[23]

## FREUD'S PSYCHOTHERAPY

Much of what we term as current psychotherapy derives in large part from Freud's psychoanalytic method. Although there have been many challenges to this method and many modifications have been offered, the essentials of Freud's psychoanalytic method have influenced and still profoundly influence most psychotherapists.

*Free-Association* is the basic rule of psychoanalytic psychotherapy. It requires the patient to verbalize every thought, feeling, and memory that comes to his mind regardless of how insignificant, painful, or embarrassing it is. The treatment situation is structured so as to "leave the patient . . . alone with his thoughts" as much as possible.[3] This technique tends to encourage the emergence of repressed memories and other unconscious material.

*Dream-analysis* is another major technique for acquiring access to the unconscious of the patient. Freud referred to dreams as "the royal road to the unconsicous." Since every dream is always the "product of highly idiosyncratic unconscious systems",[20] and is multiply-determined, it can be understood on many levels simultaneously, and may offer the therapist and the patient an entry into the patient's buried needs and conflicts.

*Interpretation* of the psychodynamic meaning of the patient's productions is the hallmark of psychoanalytic psychotherapy and its goal is the development of insight.[3]

*Working-through* describes the phenomenon that people learn slowly and that it takes time to give up resistances to established patterns of behavior and thought. The same issues, fears, and decisions must be discussed and rediscussed between patient and therapist before they can be assimilated and integrated.

Two of the most important concepts of Freudian psychotherapy are *resistance* and *transference*. *Resistance* refers to those forces within the personality which fight change and champion the status quo. The individual offers id resistances by refusing to give up primitive and infantile satisfactions (e.g., thumbsucking and other immature sexual practices); superego resistances take the form of obeying parental injunctions because the patient does not want to give up his attachments to parental introjects; ego resistances are those forces which defend against the recognition of painful thoughts, perceptions, and memories. Much of psychotherapeutic work within a Freudian orientation is an attempt to help the patient understand and eventually give up his resistances.[3]

*Transference* refers to the feelings, thoughts, fears, and wishes that the patient ascribes to the therapist. They are irrational elements carried over from other relationships, particularly relationships from the past. According to Freud a great deal of psychotherapeutic work should be devoted to an examination of the patient's transference reactions because an understanding of their distortions will yield to an understanding of the patient's conflicts that propel his neurosis.[22, 25]

## EXTENSIONS OF FREUD'S METAPSYCHOLOGICAL APPROACH

Since Freud's monumental discoveries, there have been several other writers whose contributions have enriched the psychoanalytic theory of personality and also undergird our orientation to the patient who participates in conjoint therapy. The ego psychologist Heinz Hartmann (1894–1970) introduced several concepts, some of which we will review because of their pertinence to our work.

*Social compliance* implies that one can never divorce the human organism from his environment for he is always affecting it and being affected by it. For Hartmann, any change in the person will *always* induce changes in his family and other key relationships.[13, 14]

Another of Hartmann's contributions was a further elucidation of the ego and ego functions. He pointed out that the strength of the individual's ego functions is always relative to the person's age, the environment in which he dwells, his key relationships, and his constitutional equipment. Furthermore, unconscious ego operations are manifested in a myriad of ordinary, day-by-day, characteristic ways of functioning such as might appear in therapy groups.[13-15]

One of Hartmann's major concepts is that in the process of development and socialization parts of the ego which are initially involved in conflict may show a *"change of function."*[13] For example, a child may utilize part of the ego to defend himself against anal matters by being clean, orderly, punctilious, etc. These character traits may eventually become part of the character and be *"conflict free"*. Hartmann distinguished *"primary autonomous ego functions"*, that is, those present at birth or soon after, from *"secondary autonomous ego functions"* which mature subsequently as a result of change of function. The stability of secondary autonomous zones can be measured by its *"resistivity to regression."*[14]

Surpassing Freudian theory in certain respects, Hartmann's ego psychology not only is interested in how the human personality deals with the complicated network of forces and counterforces of instinct and superego but is always tuned in to the person's larger sociocultural environment. An assessment of the patient and his social situation based on Freud's concepts alone may lose sight of the family unit and may tend to omit significant socio-psychological or situational factors. In helping individuals cope with their day-to-day family life, work, marriage, illness, loss, and other sources of stress, we can look at these dimensions of living as ego tasks and manifestations of the operations of the ego organization, as well as derivatives of drives and other psychic forces.[24]

The concepts of primary and secondary autonomous ego functions have had tremendous impact on psychotherapeutic practice. First, by being very specific about the patient's ego functions—memory, frustration tolerance, relations to others, etc.—the therapist can more specifically assess degrees of adaptability. Once recognizing which ego function or functions are impaired, the therapist can better determine where and what in the individual and in his social milieu are contributing to the dysfunctioning. Second, by recognizing that certain character traits such as orderliness, punctiliousness, curiosity etc., might be secondarily autonomous, the therapist now realizes that there is no need to explore these traits in treatment; they are "conflict free."[14]

By relating to what is "conflict free" in the patient, this may be the part of the patient's personality which can be utilized to form a therapeutic alliance with the therapist, so that patient, therapist, and co-patients can work together to resolve what is maladaptive.[10]

By utilizing the concept of the ego in the treatment situation, the therapist recognizes that if several of the patient's ego functions are weak, the patient will feel strong anxiety if too much dynamic material is probed or if he is confronted by interpretations which his ego cannot master.[19, 21] Therefore, by assessing ego functions, the therapist can plan differential treatment that will relate to the patient's unique capacities to handle frustration, bear anxiety, and relate to the therapist and others in the treatment setting.[22, 23]

Quite akin to some of Hartmann's concepts are those of Anna Freud. Miss Freud emphasized that one of the ego's operations necessary for adaptation is to defend against anxiety. Anxiety may erupt when id impulses appear dangerous, superego commands are too ominous, or environmental threats are too frightening. Defenses such as denial, projection, and introjection reversal are utilized to block the anxiety.[18] What is an important implication of Anna Freud's work is that for many patients the treatment situation may appear dangerous and they may deny their need for it, project their difficulties on to others (the therapist, other patients, family members, etc.), or utilize other defensive maneuvers. Consequently, in order to help many patients feel comfortable in the treatment situation, as Spotnitz, Nelson, and others have averred, their defenses (resistances) must be supported and reinforced.[19, 21, 23]

As will be demonstrated in later chapters, it is important, particularly during the early phases of treatment, for the patient to have his habitual defensive responses protected by the therapist; otherwise, the patient may very well flee from the treatment situation.[22, 23]

Consolidating our psychosocial orientation to the human being is the work of Erik Erikson. In formulating his epigenetic principle that the human organism has a maturational timetable, Erikson implies that the human being not only unfolds according to predetermined phases from its biological beginnings through various stages of maturation, but that human maturation cannot be viewed apart from the social context in which it transpires. For every maturational stage or "psychosocial crisis", there always appears a "Radius of Significant Relations" who aid, abet, or hinder the organism's coping with and resolving specific life tasks.[4, 5]

Each item in Erikson's eight stages* should not be regarded as a discrete unit but needed for a healthy and mature personality. For example, in order to develop a coherent sense of "autonomy", the individual has to be able to essentially "trust" first. Each ego state (trust, autonomy, etc.) is related to all others and depends on the proper development of its predecessor. Furthermore, each ego state exists in some form before its critical time for development arrives, e.g., although autonomy does not come to the fore until the second stage, its rudimentary strivings may be seen from birth.[4, 5]

Erikson uses the term crisis "to connote not a threat of catastrophe but a turning point and a crucial period of increased vulnerability and heightened potential,"[4] i.e., the maturing individual has a task to resolve. The crisis implies that there is a danger that the growing organism can be stunted in his maturation if crucial biological, psychological, and social factors do not appropriately coalesce in the task's resolution. The task also presents the opportunity to enlarge the individual's repertoire of social, interpersonal, psychological, and intellectual skills.

According to Erikson the dynamic interplay between

*Erikson's eight stages or life tasks (psychosocial crises) are trust vs. mistrust, autonomy vs. shame and doubt, initiative vs. guilt, industry vs. inferiority, identity vs. identity diffusion, intimacy and solidarity vs. isolation, generativity vs. self absorption, and integrity vs. despair.

the individual and his environment is such that the human organism can retreat to older ego states when more advanced tasks are too anxiety provoking and/or the environment and significant others pose threats to his psychic equilibrium.

In attempting to help an individual in a therapeutic situation, Erikson sees the interpersonal encounter as characterized by a "human immediacy." The total person emerges as more than a diagnostic label, a unit in a system, or a statistic. For Erikson, the sphere of attention in therapy is life itself with a particular concentration on the life tasks the individual is not able to resolve by himself. With this perspective, "seemingly malignant disturbances appear to be more ably treated as aggravated life crises rather than as diseases subject to routine diagnosis."[6]

Applying Erikson's perspective to psychotherapy it would appear that the therapist can regard himself as one of the significant persons in the patient's social radius who should be able to help him cope with a specified life task. Furthermore, the therapist can conceptualize his own professional role-set as involving unique behaviors of his own in order to be the appropriate significant other that will enhance psychosocial growth. The task at hand may require the therapist to be the trusting mother, the father that promotes initiative or with the help of a group to be the leader that helps the patient find his own identity.[24]

## EXTENSIONS OF FREUD'S PSYCHOTHERAPY

Although Freud's system of psychotherapy has influenced virtually every clinician who has engaged in the practice of treatment, other noteworthy contributions have been made, some of which have influenced the theoretical underpinning of our own work in conjoint therapy.

Since Freud's monumental discoveries, most of those

who have explicated their views on psychotherapy have focused largely on the experiential aspects of the therapy. For example, in 1925 two psychoanalysts who were students of Freud, Ferenczi and Rank, emphasized an "emotional experience" in the therapy in lieu of an intellectual, genetic understanding of the patient's neurotic symptoms and character problems.[7, 8] Because they were quite convinced that an emotional experience for the patient should replace the search for memories and intellectual reconstruction, they took the position that "the doctor must let himself go," because if the therapist "achieved the control of everything in his actions and speech and also in his feelings" he might become "too abrupt and repellent" thus retarding the development of an emotionally significant relationship or transference.[8]

Continuing the theme of therapy as an emotional experience, Otto Rank in the late 1920s emphasized that everything that occurs in the psychotherapeutic encounter should be considered, first and foremost, as a phenomenon of transference, a combination between repeating something from the past and reacting to something in the current situation. To understand transference phenomena and changes on the part of the patient, Rank averred that "much more attention should be directed to the very primitive forms of relationships such as that between a mother and her child."[7]

Alfred Adler, in the late 1920s and early 1930s focused on the experiential aspects of psychotherapy. In consonance with his conviction that most, if not all, patients who seek psychotherapy suffer from unique feelings of inferiority, he cautioned the therapist to approach each individual patient in a different way, just as he would nonpatients. The ideal therapeutic situation, according to Adler, was that patient and therapist sit face-to-face as equal fellow men. To assist the patient in overcoming his neurotic distortions Adler felt that the experience of equality in the therapy would be a strong contribution towards the patient's recovery.[1]

Alexander and French in the 1940s developed a construct, "the corrective emotional experience," as a paramount aim in treatment. "The therapist must decide carefully what attitude he must take to best further his purpose." By providing a corrective relationship for the patient, the therapist offers attitudes and interpretations that contrast markedly to those that the patient experienced with his parents and other key figures in his past. "By his own attitude and by his interpretations, the therapist provides a corrective experience for the patient in a new relationship."[2]

Seeing most psychosocial difficulties as emanating from faulty interpersonal relationships, Harry Stack Sullivan took the position that *both* patient and therapist respond to each other in terms of their mutual personalities and behavior. Like Alexander and French, Sullivan contended that for a patient to be helped, he needed a complimentary relationship with the therapist who would attempt to meet previously unmet psychosocial needs.[24] Sullivan introduced the idea that the therapist is not only an observer but a human participant in the encounter and his personality has to be reckoned with by both actors in the interpersonal encounter.[24]

In recent decades the experiential approach continues to be emphasized. Moreno, for example, has pointed out that "the personality of the therapist is his skill" and that the therapist's expression of his personality is the foundation of sound psychotherapy.[16] In existential psychotherapy, there is an emphasis on the "here and now" and the spontaneity of the therapeutic relationship. "There is a striving also for an equality and a tendency to have the situation rather unstructured. An affective honesty is paramount and the focus is on the gross lack of communication, our identity, our relation to others and our place in the total stream of existence."[17]

## AN ORIENTATION TO THE PATIENT AND HIS THERAPY

Combining Freud's metapsychology and some of the notions of the ego psychologists we have reviewed as well as those who consider psychotherapy fundamentally an experience, we are now in a position to state our own orientation to those individuals we work with in conjoint therapy. When an individual is experiencing psychosocial difficulties and expresses them through neurotic symptomology and other forms of maladaptation, it is our contention that his psychosocial processes have either regressed to or are fixated at a childhood level of development. Either the individual has experienced severe amounts of anxiety which make his usual level of functioning too difficult and consequently he returns to where life was easier (regression); or else the patient has never grown up at all (fixation). In either case, the individual has not been able, or is not able currently, to master a maturational task.[4, 21, 23]

Because our orientation states that the patient has certain maturational needs unfulfilled, he emerges in the therapeutic encounter as a child who needs experiences that will help him master a developmental task. The therapist, like the parent, must provide the appropriate experiences of frustration and gratification depending on where the patient is maturationally. Correct diagnosis should contain within it the maturational task or tasks that the patient cannot cope with alone. For example, if the maturational need requires feeding, then the therapist must offer verbal forms of feeding (e.g., praise, overt interest). If the patient is depressed, as another example, the maturational need for the patient is, in all likelihood, to discharge verbal aggression at the therapist and/or group members. As the developing child needs different environmental responses at different stages of maturation, so too, the patient at one stage of treatment may need praise and support from his therapist, and at another confrontation by peers.

As we intend to demonstrate in the following chapters, conjoint therapy offers experiences, we believe, which enhance maturation. It affords the patient opportunities to learn to transact with himself and others, using one experience to supplement the other. It rests on a Freudian metapsychological approach to the patient and is buttressed by our understanding of the ego and ego functions and maturational needs of the patient. With our understanding of the patient, the group experience and individual psychotherapy are conjointly designed to help the patient climb the psychosocial ladder of maturation.

# Chapter 2

# THE THERAPEUTIC RATIONALE FOR CONJOINT TREATMENT

What Freud[3] discovered in his explorations was that human beings share a similar emotional growth pattern. First, we develop feelings and attitudes toward our mothers or mother figures; as our awareness widens, we include our fathers and siblings; as we mature then our responses open up into the ever-enlarging world around us. As Rickman[10] put it, we pass from a "one body to a two body on to a three body interaction until we move into the multibody environment" of everyday reality.

Conjoint treatment, where the patient participates in individual psychotherapy and group therapy with two different therapists, is an attempt to replicate this movement. The first, or mothering, stage—in which the patient can reexperience the needs and feelings that are elicited by the complete dependence on one significant figure—is seen in the individual session. The group experience reflects the second stage, wherein the paternal figure, brothers, sisters, and other members of the extended family enter the emotional picture. The group analyst may become the imagined father; the group as a whole, the primitive mother; and the members, other members of the family. But the group analyst dominates the scene and dwarfs the others in the mind of the patient. The alternate session, when the members meet without the group analyst, represents the third state of maturation.[1] Here all the conflicts and confrontations reminiscent of the frustrations and satisfactions of family life are played out again, but with two differences: first, there is no obvious authority figure, and second, friends, grandmothers, teachers, uncles, and other figures important in the formative years take on influential roles. Peers shape each other's responses and tastes.

Initially, as conjoint workers, we attempted an exact replaying of the developmental drama. The prospective patient was interviewed by either the group analyst or the individual analyst and was referred to one-to-one treatment with the understanding that he would enter group treatment at some future date.

Once a transference had been established and resistances to the group experience explored and resolved, the patient entered group treatment concurrently with his individual work. As he progressed and moved into the oedipal difficulties, he was transferred to a group that also had alternate sessions. As his autonomous functioning increased, his individual sessions became fewer in number until, when they had all but ceased, he was "graduated."[7]

During the 18 years that the authors have been practicing this form of treatment, we have found it unnecessary to superimpose an inflexible template on all patients. Many people can enter all three settings at once and benefit from the multiple experience. Under the impact of two analysts and a number of peer siblings the patient confronts the same problems in each setting.

A 35-year-old film producer seemed to present a different person in each of three different settings. In his individual hour he was concerned with his critical mother, whose love he was driven to win with big productions and other outward signs of worldly success. No matter what he did, he experienced the analyst as difficult to please.

At the same time, in the regular group sessions he competed with the group analyst. Toward his fellow members in general, he appeared more perceptive than the leader, with the women he acted more gentle and sensitive, and with his male peers, more supportive, particularly if they showed any rebelliousness toward the leader.

In the alternate meetings he provoked confrontations and was daring. He said things other members might hesitate to say for fear of hurting the feelings of others. He was not above a little acting-out to seduce the women or "to put the men down."

Much later in his therapy his pervasive problem with the authority figures dominated his communications in all three settings. In each it was examined from a different perspective.

His peers in the alternate session kept bringing to his attention his covert conflicts with the group analyst and drawing parallels and comparisons between his abrasive behavior toward them and the group leader's behavior. They kept showing him how he behaved in an arbitrary fashion with them, the very thing he accused the group analyst of doing. In the regular sessions, the group analyst aided the process by scrutinizing every challenge the patient offered to his "dictatorial" manner. The producer himself used his individual sessions to probe into the perplexing problem of his contrary attitudes and activities in other settings.

As with all forms of treatment, conjoint work has its assets and liabilities. On the positive side, advantages and indications may be found in the experiential richness of multiplicity. Instead of one stimulus, one response, or one possiblility for exploration, confrontation, analysis, and resolution, many are available, and more than one may often be needed. It has appeared to us through the years that almost all patients benefit from this exposure. For some types of personalities it seems almost a necessity.

## THE USE OF MULTIPLE TRANSFERENCES

Take the case in which there exists more than one ongoing transference, a phenomenon that has been frequently reported.

Grete Bibring-Lehner [1] in 1936 described a patient who had discontinued treatment with his previous male analyst, whom he had identified in his mind with his father. Because of this, functioning appropriately and profitably in the analytic setting had become too crippling and painful for him. Some time later he resumed analysis, this time with Bibring-Lehner. He at once identified her with his mother, a role in which he perceived the analyst as not at all threatening because he had felt free and easy with his original maternal figure.

He would rail against his former therapist in disappointment and express many fantasies of defiance and revenge. Then he would expand on how superior Bibring-Lehner was as an analyst.

All seemed to be going well until she realized that the patient was trying to keep the negative aspects of his present relationship fastened onto the first analyst. His praises were being used to conceal doubts about Bibring-Lehner that were beginning to arise. To circumvent a sudden outbreak of treatment-destructive acting-out, Bibring-Lehner examined every reproach leveled at the previous analyst from the viewpoint of reality. Then she established some connection with similar events or responses in the patient's early years. Through review, reflection, and reevaluation she helped the patient separate the past from the present. The illusory quality of his reservations and doubts evaporated.

One of Bibring-Lehner's recommendations was that an analyst sacrifice his therapeutic ambitions and act in a professionally responsible manner by arranging for the referral of any patient in the state of intractable resistance to an analyst of the opposite sex. This would reduce the intensity of the ego resistance and, at the same time, increase the patient's willingness to cooperate with the analytic process. When the therapeutic modality restricts the therapeutic progress, Bibring-Lehner's recommendation is a valuable one. Fine[2] too has reported that sex can play a decisive role in resolving tenacious transference resistance, and has recommended that patients with an unmanageable positive transference be transferred to an analyst of the opposite sex.

In the authors' approach, however, we have not found it necessary to terminate the treatment with any one analyst because of such blockage of progress. When one of us has limited leverage with a patient because of the transference, the other or the group members tend to have greater access to him. Nor have we found it necessary to switch many patients to an analyst of the opposite sex.[2] Within the three settings we structure (individual, group, and alternate), there is inevitably someone who can approach the patient in a conflict-free way. On the rare occasions when a patient uses both of us in a grossly distorted way, we switch the focus onto the group as the place where objective observers can sift out the interpersonal intricacies and penetrate to the reality of the situation.

Multiple transferences occur all the time in the group setting. Each peer represents a different aspect of a parental introject. One member may be perceived as the imperious father, another the amiable father, another the withdrawn father, and still another the raging father. All are parts of the original figure, which has been split into workable segments with the happy result that feelings and attitudes toward the figure in each state can be grappled with and resolved by the yet uncertain ego.

There are times when an entire group can become one transferential figure. The patient may have undergone a series of traumas which are difficult to resolve in the shared treatment setting. One patient had a violent reaction to the group when it coalesced, for him, into an early classroom experience where the teacher had repeatedly labeled him as stupid. To another, the group became a brutal family setting in which he had repeatedly been humiliated by parents and siblings. Anything the group analyst or the members said was experienced by the patient as degrading, and he was unresponsive to their interventions. But the individual therapist was seen as a kindly grandfather. With him the patient could examine the past brutalities and separate them from the present distortions.

In all, it is as if the toxic charge is taken out of a crippling relationship when it is examined in a relatively unthreatening area of another environment. Thus, in conjoint treatment a patient inaccessible to influence in one setting becomes accessible to influence in another.

The existence of multiple transferences also permits the therapist to work for an intense level of transference without the danger of premature termination of treatment. In one setting the patient can discuss with the therapist his fantasies of flight or his overt intentions of dropping out of another setting. This can be instrumental in resolving the treatment-destructive tendencies as the following demonstrates:

> In a screening interview, a 35-year-old claim adjuster mentioned that this was his sixth attempt at therapy in 11 years. When questioned further he revealed that previous treatments had proceeded harmoniously until the therapist turned out to be like his carping mother.
>
> He had left home at the age of 14 because of her and was not going to spend "one single second in the presence of anyone like her." Yet his presenting complaint had nothing to do with the historical pattern. It was focused on superiors who tended to find fault with him.
>
> He had been through two marriages and five jobs. In each alliance the partner or superior had tended to evolve

into a critical figure. He had begun to sense that it had something to do with himself. It was, he thought, either a lack of good judgment on his part or an inability to predict how people were going to behave when he got close to them.

He reported that his best moments were with his peers. He had a history of positive experiences with people his own age in settings ranging from the familial (his cousins), to a Boy Scout troop, basketball team, fraternity, and bowling club.

He was placed in group treatment first. He at once impressed his peers as agreeable and alive. His intelligent contributions were respected. At both the regular and alternate sessions he was admired for his light-heartedness. He created in others the feeling that life was not a serious, heavy burden. A powerful positive relation developed between the group and himself. There were few abrasive clashes with the leader, for he generally regarded the latter as part of the group in general.

His progress was rapid. He reported that his home life kept improving, particularly his relations with his children. The only marring touch was his occasional reporting that he was discontented with his supervisor, with whom he was having severe "run-ins." The group seemed to offer little help in this matter. He was excellent in the field because he was among "people of his own kind," but he would run into trouble in the office. It tended to be over some "insignificant detail," such as, the way he interrupted a superior. He attributed his problems to office politics.

He agreed to enter individual treatment concurrently to explore the matter further. From the first session he was aloof and reserved with the conjoint analyst. He appeared to be waiting for something to happen. Since the therapist played a quiet role with him, the patient could find little fault with his functioning except for his silence. Then the patient began to test the analyst. He would ask a question, and no matter how the analyst responded, would find the response evasive, "beside the point," "inept," or "off target."

The relationship soon came to an impasse. He declared in one session that a critical problem had arisen in his job. There was no question that he was the best car accident assessor in his section, yet his "incompetent" superior had promoted a junior man with less experience and ability over him. He was preparing to go over his supervisor's head to protest, an admittedly dangerous procedure. How could he do it without getting his "walking papers?"

He began to press the analyst for help. The analyst suggested that perhaps it was not his work that was tripping him up; he seemed competent enough. It might be more helpful to look at his interpersonal functioning. How could this situation have developed? The patient became agitated, and said he had no ideas about it and insisted that the analyst elaborate on this point. The analyst indicated that the patient might be communicating his reservations to his supervisor and testing tendencies directly and indirectly, as he tended to do in his therapeutic sessions. By someone who did not understand him, this pattern might be viewed as provocative, contemptuous, or even insolent.

At this piece of information the patient lost his temper. He asserted that he did not need criticism now, he needed help, and if it was not forthcoming, he was not going to waste his time here any more. He thereupon stormed out of the room.

He opened the next group session by asking the leader for a new individual therapist—someone who was helpful and, above all, uncritical. The members wanted to know what had happened. He gave them a sketchy report. They were confused by it, and several wanted to know exactly what the analyst had said. Objectively and sympathetically, they obliged him to go over the story in detail. They dissected and questioned every statement and response.

It soon became apparent to them—as they made clear to him—that he viewed as demeaning any comment from a superior which was not laudatory. The closer he got to such a person, the more he unconsciously incited or challenged him and experienced him as critical, no matter how that person responded.

By the end of the group session, the members were urging him to return to the analyst and discuss his reactions further. What followed were upsetting individual sessions in which the patient could barely restrain himself from walking out again, each of which was followed by supportive group exploratory sessions in which the members would go over what happened. The group leader aided the process each time by helping the members focus on the parallels between the individual analyst and the patient's mother and how they all led to his breaking up his relationships.

Every time the transference resistance peaked in the individual session, with the patient threatening to leave, the analyst would agree that perhaps he was being irritating or provocative and asked the patient how he could be less so. He never questioned any of the patient's distortions and his attitude was consistently nonjudgmental. He avoided initiating any exploration and followed the patient's lead at all times.

His unqualified acceptance put the patient in an untenable position. But the analyst would leave it to the group to help the patient understand how he could feel so criticized and yet rationally also see that this was not what was actually happening.

In three months much of his tendency to act out his rage was resolved. It would occur intermittently, but the patient would deal with it in the individual sessions when it arose. After a while he was comfortable enough so that the analyst could say anything without risking the possibility that the patient would storm out of the session. Concomitantly the patient's problem with his supervisor eased. The claim adjuster began, in this relationship, to display much of the same ease he displayed with the group members.

## THE USE OF MULTIPLE OBSERVERS

With many a patient, an analyst's efforts may be of little avail until the patient reports that an outside source, which has no connection with what was taking place in the office, has commented on the same thing that the analyst has been pointing out for months. It is as if all the therapeutic work up to that point had, at best, put the patient in a state of readiness to hear it from another source. Surprised, puzzled, and occasionally gratified, the patient may turn into a cooperative ally overnight.

To patients like that, observations and comments coming simultaneously from several different persons can be singularly efficacious. When remarks similar in nature come from a number of people with a variety of backgrounds, histories, and views of life, the patient's ego is forced to pay heed. It is impressive to see how a person who will ignore a comment by his wife will be affected when confirming remarks are made by his elevator man, barber, or secretary. Their influence is powerful because all these sources of comment are unrelated and they seem to him to have less investment than his wife in manipulating or modifying him.

In conjoint treatment, the patient cannot deny the reality of his behavior or attitude as each observer reinforces the other with an undeniable cumulative effect. What is more, each observer is meaningful to the patient—as the transferential brother, the benevolent science teacher, the reminiscent war buddy, the bountiful grandmother. The following case history illustrates this:

A 30-year-old bookkeeper, timid and withdrawn, kept describing her lonely lot to her individual analyst. Repeatedly, she would go through the endless list of her deficiencies: she was not good-looking, witty, intellectual, sexual; men ignored her; and so on.

To the analyst, who had seen her over a period of three years, these claims were a mass of contradictions. The patient could not imagine that anyone would take an interest in her insipid chatter, yet when relaxed she would often come up with a perfect bon mot to sum up the activities of someone in her office. She showed flashes of sparkling wit and had a fresh way of looking at mundane activities. She insisted she could not hold a five-minute discussion on any subject, yet spoke fluently about politics and social events, attended plays on and off Broadway, and knew about art exhibitions on Madison Avenue and in Soho. She held that she could do nothing, yet she arranged her own travel every year to some music festival in the United States or Europe. She enrolled in an art school and demonstrated above-average gifts as a water-colorist. She maintained that she had no special physical endowments, but under her drab, unshapely clothes she appeared to have a trim figure, and if one looked past her unkempt hair and nervous twitching one could make out attractive features.

All attempts to bring these ignored attributes to her attention were brushed aside. If the analyst pointed out any of them at the appropriate moment, she would stiffen, and then declare that he was "spoofing" her. He was like one of her foster mothers who had always tried to build her up and make her believe in qualities that were not there. She had no confidence in his comments. She felt he made them because he was paid to do so. She would become silent and withdrawn in disappointment and distrust. Only when he agreed with her that she had little that was worthwhile would she open up again and talk freely.

One day she was bemoaning the lack of friends and thanking the stars that at least there was analysis for people like her who needed "confession closets where they can weave their cloistered cobwebs." The analyst suggested that she consider entering a group of peers with another analyst. She was most reluctant to do so, and resisted this idea for weeks. Only when she was firmly convinced he would not stop seeing her did she consent.

She entered a group of sophisticated teachers, therapists, and writers. Because the men were involved in a volatile confrontation with each other and because she said little at the outset, the members gave her only nodding attention. This confirmed all her worst conceptions about herself. She stormed at her individual analyst and called him brutal and cruel for subjecting her to this latest humiliation. Nevertheless, she attended the group sessions punctually and regularly, and watched the interchanges of the members with silent fascination.

For two months she neither progressed nor regressed in the group, but in her individual sessions she was preoccupied with all its interactions, brilliantly describing the members. Though she denied any feelings for them, her communications indicated great admiration and envy.

The turning point came about almost casually. A male member was describing the shimmering lack of definition of a female member. He could not get a solid sense of her sexuality. He said it reminded him of the painting "Nude Descending a Staircase by . . ." He paused—he could not remember the artist. The group fell silent, as none of the other members could muster the name either. In a quiet voice the patient filled the gap: "Marcel Duchamp."

All heads turned toward her, some interested and others curious. A few began to question her, and expressed surprise when she revealed that she was a bookkeeper. One of the men, who had previously reported his tendency to plan the lives of his girl friends in order to improve them, began to question her. Others joined in as aspects of her multifaceted personality appeared and disappeared. Her self-deprecating answers annoyed them. One of the women suggested a beauty parlor where she could get her hair done reasonably. "At least, you won't look like a chimney sweep!"

This suggestion brought her real fears to the surface. Earlier, her analyst had pointed out that the denial of her assets was a device to protect her against her doubts about her own sexuality. Feeling inadequate and terrified, she belittled herself in order to forestall any possibility of being exposed to a sexual advance.

She was now more amenable to working on the sexual fears in the individual session and finally took a chance on a new hairstyle. When the members saw that she was being responsive to them, others joined in with suggestions as to what dresses she might wear and where she might buy them at prices within her means. Each time she put a recommendation into action, she received positive reinforcement from the group as a whole.

In her individual sessions she revealed that she found the attention overwhelmingly gratifying, and cried most of the time. There must be something to her, or these "excellent people" would not take such an interest.

Because the group had echoed what the analyst had said, his statements now carried enormous leverage. He began to explore the details of her past with her complete cooperation. She poured out the minutiae of her early neglect. Fatherless, she had been abandoned by her mother at the age of four. Authorities shuttled her from foster home to foster home, in each of which she was the recipient of "hand-me-downs." There was no thought or plan for her future. Whatever she learned, she picked up by herself.

The only people who were interested in her in any consistent way were a few schoolmates. These girl friends formed her only enriching relationships. She would listen avidly to what they said about their lives, though she did not participate in them. The details of their dates, accomplishments, activities, and endowments had a great influence on her: she viewed them with awe and regarded them as unobtainable for her. Secretly she studied her friends' behavior and imitated it in front of a mirror, but her own sense of insignificance prevented her from using in public what she practiced in private.

Once the members of the group (her schoolmate surrogates) had reinforced what the individual analyst observed, she could trust him as someone truly interested in her. He became the mother she had never had. Everything he suggested or pointed out pervasively influenced her thinking and behavior. On the other hand, she now often saw the group analyst as being like the indifferent social workers, foster parents, or school authorities who had had no time for her. At other moments he became the wonderful father she concocted out of her daydreams and fantasies.

A woman in the group met an "exciting" man at a Club Med in Martinique. This fired the patient's interest in meeting a "real man." She did voluminous research on resorts she might go to on her vacation, what clothes she should wear there, and what situations might occur. She discussed the matter fully with her individual analyst and then discussed her decision with the group.

This became the pattern throughout the rest of her treatment. What she observed the members doing stimulated her. She would work through her feelings about them in her private sessions. Then she would air these feelings and thoughts toward the members of her group. If the members said anything similar to what the individual analyst was saying, a significant reorientation would take place in her attitude, manner, activity, or thinking.

## THE USE OF MULTIPLE INTERPRETERS

It is a common experience among therapists to find that a single interpretation, even though it is accurate, may be summarily rejected by the patient. Even when it is accepted, it may have little and quickly lost effect.

To meet this therapeutic difficulty Freud[4] developed the concept of working-through, that is, giving the same information again and again from different positions in different situations until the power of repeated education takes effect. The analyst may approach the material at one time from the ego position; at another time from that of the superego; still another from that of the id or of secondary gain. He may keep the insight in the forefront of the patient's attention and remind him that they had discussed the matter before by noting, "See, again we find you placing yourself in a position with me where I am called on to give you advice." But all this recapitulating, to get the patient to absorb and integrate the new insight, uses up a great deal of time.

In conjoint treatment, multiple interpreters take over the function of viewing and reviewing the same material or behavior. Each member uses a different language, gives insight from a different perspective, and uses the leverage of a different relationship to bring the point home. The collective force of this is more than one analyst endlessly, sometimes impotently, going over the same patterns with a particularly recalcitrant patient as the following shows:

> A highly successful 55-year-old businessman presented himself for individual treatment at the insistence of his personal physician. His symptoms were insomnia, undefined lower back pains, and "incipient ulcers." He held his 25-year-old son, who had been taken in as a junior partner in the business, to be responsible for his physical deterioration.
>
> What rapidly developed was a struggle with the analyst as to who was going to conduct the therapy. If a business issue came up at the last moment, he would have his secretary cancel the appointment. Then he would engage in a running battle about paying for the session he did not attend. He could see no problem about payment as long as the analyst received a check before the tenth of the month. If the analyst indicated he would like to be paid in person, the patient would dismiss that request as "unbusinesslike."

On the couch he talked only about his son and how "ungrateful" the boy was. "Taking on a partner was like taking on trouble." He had been a loner and had made it. He did not need family troubles in his place of business. If asked about other areas of life, he would indicate with a wave of the hand that they were not important.

Interventions about his resistances to cooperation and interpretations of them were turned aside with such phrases as, "What makes you think I act the same way outside as I do here?" or "When you get as old as I am and have gone through what I have, such things don't bother you." Any confrontation he could not handle concerning their therapeutic work together he avoided by stating that the analyst and he did not work together well, or that the analyst still had a lot to learn.

After three months of berating his fate and warding off any insight, he declared he was "getting nowhere." His ulcer was getting worse. He was taking more Valium to sleep.

The analyst suggested that what was needed was intensified treatment. Twice a week was not enough. Would he have any objection to adding a group session with an analyst who was older than himself and had a number of people near the patient's own age?

The patient thought that this was a capital idea. The new group pleased him at once. He quickly established a sense of camaraderie with two members who were his contemporaries and were also in business. He gave them his highest accolade: "Now *these* are men I could play poker with." He was moderately respectful toward the group leader, whom he regarded as successful in his profession: "Any man who runs so many groups has got to know what he is doing." To the women he was formal and condescending.

It was the younger members who created difficulties for him. He treated them as if they were children. When he was not ignoring their observations, he was interrupting their communications to each other, telling them where they missed the point, giving them directions or advice about their lives, and spelling out what they should have done and did not do.

The younger members developed intense responses to him. They projected onto him every authoritarian figure they had ever come up against in the past. At one point, when he was berating the newest member about his dress and hair style, the junior members rose up against him en masse. They called him dictatorial, rigid, pig-headed, and "twenty years behind the times." Each fed the others' anger until they all declared that he was too obnoxious to remain in their group.

At first, he successfully defended himself. But when his "poker-playing friends" quietly agreed with the assault, he became confused. He asked the leader what he thought. The group analyst explored his bewilderment and pointed out that maybe he had had a role in the response he was getting. The patient fell silent. In the following individual session he was quiet and pensive. He told the analyst he wanted to know "the truth, the whole truth." The analyst slowly reviewed the development of their own relationship, pointing to parallels in the group based on the patient's own reports. In both places the patient had behaved in the same arbitrary manner.

The effect was profound. The patient whispered, "So they're all right." After a period of silence, he began to sob. His wife was right, too. She had said he was treating his son as his father had treated him by not really giving the boy a break. He began to recount the numerous conflicts he had had with his own parents; he had finally left Poland for America because he could not stand the tyranny to which he was subjected when he worked in his father's grain mill. At the end of the session he was calmer and was resolved to see if things could not be different.

In both group and individual settings, he became more aware of himself. He would investigate other members' reactions to him and relate them to his life experiences. At home he began to heed his wife's suggestions on how to treat his son. She soon commented that he was "easier going" and was giving his son a freer hand in the business. He also began to spend time on a long-neglected hobby of building ships in bottles.

His lower back pains diminished and he began to sleep better. There was no more talk in the individual sessions about his ulcer. He was now too concerned about his misunderstandings with the women in the group.

Two years later, he confided that the most significant event in his treatment had taken place when all the important people coming from different backgrounds and positions told him the same thing at the same time "It was like an earthquake. It shook me inside out. There is a saying: when the people tell you you are drunk, go home and lie down, even if you haven't had a sip of wine. It happened to me."

## THE USE OF MULTIPLE EMOTIONAL RESOLVERS

A unique advantage of conjoint analysis is that the patient has many people helping him to resolve difficulties instead of just one, particularly on the emotional level. To understand how this works, let us review the therapeutic process.

Basically, there are three steps in analytic therapy: developing the transference, studying it—which calls for observing and investigating—and resolving it.[8] First, a patient has to develop the appropriate feelings toward his analyst; that is, the patient has to feel toward the analyst the way he felt toward significant people in his childhood when his inner growth took aberrant twists because of the relationship.[12, 13]

Analysts do not do anything but study the patient's responses until he begins to use his transference feelings to obstruct the progressive movement of the treatment. For example, instead of engaging in constructive verbal communication, he may want to go into action. He may start talking about irrelevant matters, bringing coffee, or finding pretexts to touch the analyst. In fact, he may want to communicate in any way except by the use of meaningful words. This is not desirable or indicated in analytic treatment, and is a tendency which has to be resolved. Usually, the analyst gives the patient a carefully timed interpretation at the peak of the resistance. This is successful with patients who are in the oedipal phase of treatment.

If the patient is demonstrating a preoedipal pattern, he may need emotional resolution. If the analyst can muster the right feelings with the right intensity, and it is appropriate for him to communicate them, all goes well.[12] But this is not always possible when the preoedipal aspects of a personality structure are dominant. The patient may require a wide range of meaningful responses that the analyst is not in a position to provide; or if he does provide them, he is not believed. Here the group members, unhampered by any professional considerations, can exert meaningful leverage.

A 34-year-old computer consultant sought out a group because of his "lack of roots." He had a facility for making acquaintances, and yet he said he failed to establish meaningful relationships.

The members found him pleasant enough. He was obliging, agreeable, and responsive. He would listen sympathetically to everyone, but contribute only chatter. The members could learn little about the essential person. It was difficult to know what he felt about them or anyone else in his life. He could answer all questions at great length, but eventually managed to veer off in a sterile direction.

The group, led by the analyst, once pressed him into telling them the exact nature of his social life. He had no female companionship. Each weekend he went to a ski resort, or weekend club, or took a single trip. He met new women each time, spent money liberally on them, and then tried to date them when he got back home. But the contacts faded away. The same was true with the group members. They liked him in a lukewarm way but, in spite of his charm, found themselves more interested in other members.

He was attentive and distant to the group analyst, whom he equated with his favorite teacher in junior high school.

After ten months of group treatment the analyst referred him to concurrent individual work with an "active" therapist who was interested in characterological defenses. The individual therapist investigated his behavior with singular vigor. The excessive smiling, nodding, and cliché phrases, such as "right on," were submitted to minute examination.

As the facade fell away, a secretive man emerged, a man who was painfully embarrassed to show anything about himself. While this was being explored, the patient recalled that he had played the part of an Indian guide in a Thanksgiving play at the age of seven. As he stepped forward to deliver the pipe of peace, his pants fell down. He had no underwear on. The audience, including his mother, collapsed in laughter. To compound his humiliation, in the front row he saw his father red-faced with rage and mortification at his son's bumbling. That evening at the dinner table his mother "joshed" him about the incident in front of his gleeful sisters. His father said nothing about the incident.

The patient fell silent and with growing trepidation waited for the analyst to say something. The analyst asked him questions about exposure, sexuality, and his father's feelings. From then on, the analyst's assertive stance had little effect. The patient was restrained and distant.

The individual analyst discussed this patient with his group colleague. They pooled their observations and agreed that the patient's wariness was responsible for the emotional shallowness of his relating, and that its basis was the unpredictable exposure and humiliation he thought he might experience, based on his past history. The individual analyst was now his father incarnate, whose criticism he feared, hated, and could not confront. He thought that his group peers might laugh at him. He needed a new emotional response to resolve the dilemma, and the group analyst would be the person to initiate work on it.

During one group session a member fathomed the patient's reticence behind his affability and tried to find out what was being hidden. The analyst declared that the patient did not have to say anything unless he felt comfortable. A confrontation broke out between the analyst and the members who disagreed with him. The patient was agreeably gratified by the analyst's support. He was also surprised to find someone defending his position.

Members questioned the analyst angrily. They felt that they did not know the patient. He was taking up a chair and giving little of himself. He did not seem to be getting anywhere. Why did he not try a new course of action, take a chance?

The patient, feeling that the analyst was on his side, asked what they wanted of him at the moment. One member asked him to tell the worst thing he could think of.

There was a long silence. Then the patient told the Thanksgiving tale with great feeling. He broke into tears as he described standing naked in front of the audience.

The group analyst again supported him. "That could happen to anyone. What do the rest of you think?" A woman smiled at the patient and said it reminded her of the times she gave her son a bath. If she had seen a little boy with his "tussie and his wee-wee all bare on the stage" she would have gone up and put her arms around him and "hugged him and hugged him."

A soft, relaxed look crossed the patient's face as the wariness washed away. He told her she was wonderful to say that. As the members made a partial identification with him, a great feeling of warmth went out to him. The meeting ended on a powerful new note for the patient. He had found a new home base, where acceptance had priority over imminent criticism.

He confronted his individual analyst with his disappointment at the response the analyst had given his tale, which he compared unfavorably to the group's openness. He spent stormy sessions pointing out what he perceived as the analyst's provocative obtuseness. In the group he discussed the individual analyst's responses and was accessible to the understanding the members gave him.

A more relaxed and natural person began to emerge. He was quicker to flare up and was less hesitant to reveal what he felt about his co-members. This new openmindedness reflected itself in his real life. He reported joining a handball team at the YMCA and finding a friend with whom he could share common interests.

As can be seen, patients need to receive the right feelings when they are reactivating the pathological conditions which shaped their present inadequate functioning patterns. Since somebody has to provide these feelings, no assembly of people is better equipped to do so than fellow group members who have so many different emotional responses available.

This is an important factor in selection. A patient

should enter a group that can give him the kind of feelings he needs. A group of schoolteachers in their twenties might be totally inadequate to the task of sensing and meeting the needs of a 60-year-old immigrant woman who has just lost her husband and is trying to adjust to a new set of realities. What is more, maturational feelings have to be provided by peers at the right time, that is, when the member has developed a transference resistance.

## THE USE OF MULTIPLE THERAPEUTIC SETTINGS

In the interest of self-protection, many patients restrict their activities, minimize any jarring social encounters, and tread cautiously through their circumscribed worlds. The relief from anxiety which this isolation affords them reinforces this constraint.

They rationalize this monastic existence both to themselves and to anyone who comes in contact with them. They develop ingenious ways of side-stepping situations which they feel might be dangerous. Their arguments have a logic that is self-convincing. If these rationalizations lose their validity under analytic scrutiny, the patients will muster new ones or mobilize other defense mechanisms. If they can no longer deny the analyst's view of reality, they come to a standstill in and out of treatment.

They neither go forward nor backward, and work to keep things as they are. To ensure this inviolability, they may dress the analyst in the robes of some weak figure in the past who had little influence on them. They feel as if going to their analytic sessions is analogous to paying homage to a religious ritual in which they no longer believe.

Such a patient talks interminably about the disability that brought him to therapy until it absorbs all his psychic energy. Because he has semi-successfully dealt with the disability by limiting his exposure to any external stimuli which might open new and seemingly dangerous avenues of experience, he is left with nothing to talk about but his pervasive preoccupation. The analytic hours become barren. The process takes on a circular character. It is apparent that though he may suffer, he has no intention of giving up what small gain he has managed to wrest from his wretched restrictions. It is a fruitless endeavor to convince him that the relinquishment of any secondary gain might in the end lead to a fulfilling life.

In order to give the patient analytic mobility, it is helpful to consider the multiplicity of settings offered by conjoint treatment. In these separate arenas, the same pathological pattern can be examined from continuously different positions. The ego is kept in a state of disequilibrium. On this psychological shuttle the patient can no longer limit the amount of environmental stimuli. Where one setting is ineffective for a particular theme, the other may be very successful therapeutically; what one setting initiates, the other may expand.

When each setting is working in a rhythmic interplay, each echoing the other as they operate in unconscious tandem, the effect cannot be denied. Rocklike resistances melt and are replaced by heated communications covering every area of the patient's life.

A 42-year-old member of the bar devoted every evening to dedicated research on a mammoth history of the Roman legal system, but he never began to write it. Information was collected, collated, organized, and reorganized. This nocturnal modus vivendi was the solution to a problem that had vexed him for many years and finally forced him into treatment.

He was independently wealthy and connected to socially prominent families. With a first-class mind, and striking features, he was considered a very eligible bachelor and had been for many years. In his office he could talk freely to a woman within the framework of his profession. In fact, he presented himself as a relaxed gentleman of ineffable charm.

But should he inadvertently bump into the same woman in a restaurant, he would mumble helplessly. His breathing would become difficult, his heartbeat would double, and his only thought was to escape.

His puzzled relatives and his enchanted clients were only aware of his assets. They did not know he suffered from overwhelming anxiety. For years they sought to inveigle him into cocktail parties, concerts, or dinners where they might introduce him to eligible women. At the last moment, or at least close to it, something unfortunate would occur. He would have a car accident, develop a high fever, get caught in a critical conference, or meet with some other unforseen misfortune. If his excuse was checked out, it would be found to be legitimate.

He attended all his analytic sessions punctually and declared sincerely that he would like to marry and have children to carry on the family name. Any insight his analyst offered, he understood and politely accepted, and nothing happened. He spent his analytic hours talking about his clients, the women he met in his office, his magnum opus, and, last but not least, his anxiety.

One day the analyst confronted him on the subject of his determination to avoid social relationships, and suggested that since they were not making any progress the treatment should be terminated. The announcement unsettled the patient. He felt that as long as he was being analyzed he was doing something. If he stopped, his future would be totally bleak.

The analyst indicated that if he wanted to continue, he would have to focus on his major problem. It would be helpful if he met some women socially. This idea amplified the patient's anxiety. He could see that talking in circles about the problem was getting him nowhere. He could not bring himself to contact women, however, because he thought he would make a fool of himself.

The analyst suggested that perhaps he needed to meet women in a structured situation, such as a group, before he sought them out socially. While the analyst did not conduct groups himself, he could send him to someone who did. The thought alternately intrigued and terrified the patient. The analyst reassured him. He could always drop out and return to their old schedule. Seeing another therapist who could study his behavior in vivo could be an asset. He would be viewed from a new angle; new information could be culled from direct observation; and the group therapist could step in to protect him if matters got out of hand. After much weighing of the pros and cons, the patient agreed to give it a try.

His initial aloof silence fascinated the members. The first communication from a woman astonished him. She told him that she sensed that he was not so much scared of her as scared that he might kill her.

When he reported this "shocking bit of news" to his individual analyst, he was reminded that he had been told this a number of times before. He had no recollection of it. The analyst suggested that perhaps it had more meaning to him this time because it came from the lips of a woman. The patient was struck by the disparity. Why was this so? What emerged was that the analyst played the role of his father, a weak, shadowy figure who had little direct influence on his life.

A few sessions later he tried to pursue the "killer" observation with the woman who had mentioned it. Her response was succinct. "So you want to murder me. What's the big deal?" Baffled, he spent his private sessions trying to reason out what she meant. In the process he began to experience some anger. The discovery of his hate feelings kept him in a high state of excitement. During this time he did not overtly respond to the women in the group. He was superficially cool to them, although inwardly quaking with fear and hatred. But he used his private sessions to sort out his thoughts from his actions and his feelings from his impulses. The fact that a feeling, no matter how strong, did not mean that he would do something about it, was revolutionary to him.

Matters came to a head with the announcement that a new woman would be introduced into the group. He vehemently protested. He told the analyst that there were too many women in the group as it was. When the other men supported the introduction of a woman, he became silent.

He did not appear for her first session with the group. His answering service left a message with the analyst's service that he was detained in Dallas. When he arrived for the following session, the group analyst led the members in inquiring what had happened. The facts were as stated: He had gone to close a deal in natural gas. The signing of the contract could have been completed in good time, but he had told himself that the matter called for delicacy and that delicacy required time. The new element in his usual explanatory process was that he recognized this as a rationalization. He knew he was timing his moves with the day of the group session in mind. He wanted to avoid the anxiety attendant to meeting a new member.

The woman asked what he thought of her. His voluble reply was critical and negative and included his expectation that she would reject him. Group members asked him how he could form all these opinions when he did not even know her. Where did all this imagining come from? He did not know.

Suddenly, he began to experience grave apprehension that increased as they asked more questions. He began to tremble visibly and kept running his tongue over his lips. The group analyst had to intervene; the members were cornering him unnecessarily. He redirected their attention to other matters. The patient sat in controlled silence, terrified and speechless.

The next day he came to his individual session with a dream: He was alone in a room with many doors. Witches glided in, swatted at him, and they vanished into thin air. He could not predict through which doors they would enter. He felt helpless, defenseless, but did not dare show it.

With the analyst's help, he explored the dream's meaning. Since his father was a chief executive of an international oil company, the patient had traveled with his family until he was old enough to be shipped off to boarding school. Each change of address meant a change of "Nanny." Some of these nursemaids were strict disciplinarians, others seductive, and others illiterate. He never knew what to expect. It kept him in a constant state of uncertainty. His mother gave her child only cursory attention and paid little attention to his fears. She told him to be "brave" and left him to the questionable mercies of strangers. In his adult years women began to represent both figures. He was terrified to meet them and furious at the imagined rejections or neglect with which they might treat him.

> With this emotional understanding, his attitude toward
> the women in the group changed. He gradually relaxed and
> could even be witty. He began to take an active interest in
> the new member, whom he found to be pleasant and sexu-
> ally attractive. He stopped working on his "opus" and wrote
> a few legal articles. Within months he reported his first date
> with a distant cousin and then further social explorations.

Through the use of the separate analytic settings—
with the added confrontations of women on his level, plus
cooperative work with his individual analyst—his ego was
kept in a state of flux. Together these two therapeutic environments helped him shed the protective patterns that nar-
rowed the social range of his life. Others have reported that
analytic resistance can be softened and shortened by the
activity of peers.[5] But the working-through and resolution
of such obstacles is greatly enhanced by conjoint collaboration.

## THE USE OF MULTIPLE COUNTERTRANSFERENCE REACTIONS

A number of patients show skill at keeping intact the secondary gains obtained from their difficulties. Chameleon-
like, their personalities take on the coloration of any
situation into which they are thrown. They seem to attune
themselves to the needs of the environment. If it calls for
attentiveness, they are attentive. If it calls for change, they
change.

Actually, the alteration is superficial. Done for defensive purposes, it is unconsciously designed to hide entrenched patterns from surveillance. The egos of such
patients are highly pliable for protection, but not in the
service of resolving difficulties.

Because the limits of their ego boundaries are poorly
defined, these patients never know where they leave off and
another person begins. Their egos move in and out of
another person's substance as if through swinging doors.

They can easily intuit the stumbling blocks of their therapists.

Once they sense the likes, dislikes, needs, kinks, unresolved conflicts, or any other latent countertransference tendencies of their analysts, their adaptive genius comes into full swing. They can metamorphose into the right person, carefully pluck the "right" emotional string, and make infinite adjustments to lead the therapy away from meaningful inner or outer confrontations. They are masters of pseudo-cooperation.

Such patients are grist for the conjoint mill, where each agent will elicit new responses. If the patient plays the labile game of unconscious manipulation and deception of those around him, sooner or later there will come a reckoning.

The comeupance happens because the patient cannot attune himself to all emotional needs of those with whom he comes into contact, particularly if there are many people in the same place at the same time. He induces in them a variety of feelings he cannot predict, control, or adapt to with protective facility.

If many objects are available for induction of feelings, such a patient's emotions and maneuvers can be studied from numerous positions and viewpoints. Some objects will respond as the patient wishes them to; others may respond in terms of the patient's introjects—mother, father, or other significant figures. Still others will be impervious to the induction. The more trained the receiver of the feeling is, the more he can use it to elucidate inner reality. As group members become more alerted to the phenomenon and receive more consensual validation of their reactions, they will trust their responses more and play them back to the inductor. Together they can put together an accurate picture of what is going on in the patient. What is critical is that instead of being reacted to, these feelings are studied and restated to the subject. Thus, the elusive member is entrapped in the network of responses laid by his peers and analysts.

These induced feelings can be labeled the objective countertransference.[9] They come in two forms: preoedipal and oedipal. In the preoedipal state, the members or analysts experience the feelings as their own. In the oedipal state, the feelings are experienced as coming from outside, foreign, even intrusive.

> At the end of a regular group session a woman declared that she would no longer attend the alternate sessions. She pointed an accusing finger at a 23-year-old actor and called him a "destructive force."
>
> The group analyst was puzzled. The member had struck him as light-hearted, humorous, and likable. If he displayed any difficulty it was that he did not take members seriously enough.
>
> But the group's view was at odds with the therapist's. They found this member irritating, contemptuous, and snobbish, particularly in alternate sessions. He was accused of pitting one member against another. The actor, shaken by the accusation, became subdued and withdrawn. The analyst supported him, saying they would talk about it at the next session. He indicated that a matter like this should be brought up at the beginning of a meeting, not at the closing.
>
> During a phone conversation between the sessions, the group analyst mentioned this development to his individual colleague and was surprised to hear the patient described as if he were another person—serious, quiet, introspective. The individual analyst added that he felt a slight compassion and sadness for him.
>
> Alerted anew by this discrepancy, they went over what they knew about the patient. He had been referred to the group by his theatrical agent to get "his head straightened out." After a meteoric start at 17 in a Broadway production, he had been dropped from one play after another while it was in rehearsal. Initially he presented himself well, gave a fine reading, but matters would get "difficult" as the time of the opening became close. He seemed to fall apart under the pressure. His latest stint in a television soap opera had been a failure for somewhat similar reasons.

The two analysts agreed that they had a complex problem on their hands. Furthermore, in the eight months the patient had been in conjoint treatment with them they had seen no evidence to confirm his occupational history, nor could they put their finger on any concrete change in him during that time. Both decided to focus on the reason for the disparity in their perceptions and feelings. Why was he responding so differently in the two settings?

In the group, the analyst began to ask the members what emotions the patient made them feel in both their regular and their alternate sessions. Once each feeling was identified, the possible reason for it was speculated upon. Each time the patient felt threatened by a member's revelation, the analyst, using the feeling induced in him, would sense it and at once lower its intensity by intellectual exploration or by treating it lightly, or would use the material to better understand the revealing member.

In another setting, the individual analyst began to play back or reflect for the patient the feelings he experienced when the patient was in session with him. At first the actor complained that this confused him, but soon he began to feel quite comfortable in the sessions when he saw that there was no pressure on him to do anything. His solemn facade faded away and other feelings appeared, which were then reflected for him. The actor felt even more at ease when he began to experience the analyst as someone quite like himself.

Through the use of their feelings and by comparing notes, the analysts began to fit the pieces together. The patient was a true actor in his real life. He was an "as if" personality who adapted himself to the emotional climate of the moment and the unconscious needs and feelings of others. Without knowing it, he reflected people he was with. In the alternate sessions he was merely expressing the hidden attitudes of the members toward each other in the absence of the authority figure. In the regular group sessions he mirrored the humor and light-heartedness of the leader. In the individual sessions he accurately reflected the essential seriousness of his analyst.

In his occupation, the same difficulty prevailed. He was easily influenced by the moods of the fellow actors, the director, the stage manager, or anyone else, whose feelings impinged on him. This controlled his functioning both off and on stage. He acted on all the feelings induced in him. There was no discrimination, individuation, or selection. When a deadline approached and dress rehearsals were going awry, he expressed everyone's panic and imminent disintegration.

This explanation was given to the group members in his presence. Though he did not grasp it, they did at once. Members took to asking him whether a particular feeling was his or whether someone else was experiencing it. His bewilderment ballooned. He felt that members were trying to drive him "crazy." The more perplexed he became, the more anxious he grew, and the more his ego balance was threatened. Often it looked as though he would fragment into irrational pieces.

The individual analyst kept him stabilized. In the individual sessions the patient was joined, supported, and mirrored. No interpretations were offered him. The analyst merely worked to resolve his objections to experiencing the emotions surging up in him. Each session became a time when the actor could release verbal violence toward the absent group and the analysts: no one understood him, he was too easy to push around, he hated everyone he ever tried to please.

In the group he became more outspoken about his own attitudes. As he became more aware of his separate existence, he began to express his aggression in a sly fashion. He started to sense his unusual gift for ferreting out the members' hidden agendas. During the regular sessions he would uncover his peers' unspoken attitudes toward the group analyst. They could not deny them, though they objected to his exposing them. But as each member's uncovered resentment joined the others', the group's aggression began to focus on the group analyst. After the analyst dealt with the shared phenomenon to the benefit of all, freeing everyone to talk about all feelings, the actor patient began to gain in status. After all, he had brought it about.

He saw that his ability to see behind people's masks could be used to his best interests. Instead of being a perpetual responsive chord, he could be a conscious activator and get rewarded for it. He became the group's pulse and catalyst. Members admired his courage in confronting secret snobbishness, covert contempt, and devious devices. When he successfully pricked the Achilles' heel of the group analyst, he was even praised.

In the individual sessions he relived some of his earliest experiences and became more object-oriented. He talked of leaving the acting profession because he felt it was not right for him and he had lost the taste for it. He played with the idea of going back to school to study directing; he even coached a few players for a "show-case," which was well received.

During all this, the conjoint analysts were in constant touch, mostly to work out the feelings the patient induced in them and track down what they meant.

Because of the group's multitude of responses, the actor's many masks could be "stripped off." Under all these personality facades lay a fragmented ego and a deeply submerged rage which had to be surfaced, verbalized, and worked through before the process of integration could take place.[6]

## MULTIPLE EGO STATES

The preceding illustration spells out a case resolved by the use of multiple countertransference reactions. It also deals with and treats one type of the phenomena known as the multiple ego state.

Many patients knowingly or unknowingly present only one side of their multi-faceted personalities to each person. The moment they meet someone, their behavior seems to take on a specific form which maintains itself with that person, no matter how conditions change. With such patients it is as if their survival depends on specializing on one response to a specific object.

At first, some of them may give an impression of normal navigating through interpersonal waters. But soon they are viewed by others not as someone to be reckoned with, but as someone who can be dismissed as shallow or limited. "Fitting in" seems more important to these people than knowing their needs, let alone fulfilling these needs.

Underneath their facades, we find these patients cowering under some psychological sword of Damocles. The responses they are giving is a thin thread that they feel may snap at any moment, with dire consequences. A dormant rage could erupt which would lead in the direction of physically assaulting the object, or they might be rejected in a way that would reanimate memories of being helpless and abandoned.

The interpersonal masks they wear are myriad. An acknowledging smile may be warding off closeness that may be equated with primitive fantasies of being devoured. A contentiousness may conceal a panic that they will be exposed as a "nothing" or even psychotic. Even in their "closet friendships" they do not dare show the full range of their feelings or opinions.

In fact, should an unacceptable emotion or idea erupt into awareness in the presence of the stimulating person, such patients experience great anxiety. While this alien threat is present in themselves, they do not trust themselves to function in their own best interests or in the best interests of the relationship. They resort to secondary defenses such as withdrawal into taciturnity, diverting the subject, or denial.

Since every day presents so many developing challenges, this one-sided way of dealing with life is inadequate. It limits flexibility and creativity. It cripples ability to meet the needs of the moment, and it severely hampers interpersonal problem solving.

For these people, conjoint treatment is often the treatment of choice. In multiple settings with multiple objects, their maladaptive mechanisms stand out in glaring relief. Their poses and operations can be scrutinized in detail.

Once they work through their old way of handling situations with specialized responses, they become more aware of their own needs, present themselves in a varied but consistent fashion, and aim for their own objectives in a more affirmative manner.

> When a 28-year-old editor was referred to her individual analyst, her previous therapist labeled her succinctly as "negative." But her new analyst was at a loss to find any indication of this state in anything she said or did. The only word he could muster to describe her was "bland."
>
> She arrived on time, paid on time, said what seemed to be on her mind—though the range of emotional charge was within fairly proscribed limits. She became animated only when discussing literature—particularly the Romantic poets and the Victorian novelists, with emphasis on the Bronte sisters.
>
> The analyst found her attractive, though demure and withdrawn. After some self-analysis, he suggested that she might be harboring positive feelings toward him. This was met with mild intellectual acknowledgment that this was possible. Then she went off into some problem with her editorial work—her primary concern.
>
> But after four months there was little perceptible movement. This was discussed several times. Each time the patient assured the analyst that this might be the case during the hour, but in her outside life things could not be going better: she had been given a raise in salary, made a senior editor, had moved to a better apartment, and was even contemplating a trip to Haiti.
>
> When the analyst wondered why he saw so little of this progress in their sessions, she pointed out that as far as she was concerned, she had been a cooperative patient. She came to appointments on time, paid her bills on time, and said what came into her mind. She was not by nature a passionate person. And she found the present treatment at least ten times superior to her last analysis, in which she had not been able to abide the presence of the therapist.
>
> She admitted there was not much dating in her life at the moment, but she never had gone out much and when she did it "was always a sexual thing." She never got far with men. They seemed to prefer "fascinating movie queens with

a million moods." Besides, they were a secondary concern now. Her energies were for the first time dedicated to her career and to personal stabilization. Men would come later.

Her arguments carried a certain conviction, and the sessions went on for three more months on the same bland note. The analyst kept searching for key feelings in her dreams, associations, and behavior. And she kept agreeing they were there.

For the analyst, the treatment had the feel of a comic reversal. Instead of the patient complaining about the analysis, it was he who was dissatisfied. At first, he attributed his discontent to his restless drive to help his patients—a resistance to objectively analyzing them which he thought he had resolved in his training analysis. But as he compared his work with the editor patient to his work with his other patients, he began to suspect that he was dealing with only one of her emotional aspects.

To test his hunch, he thought it might be a good idea to see how she behaved in another therapeutic milieu. When he suggested conjoint treatment to her, her objections were mild but firm. She saw no reason for it. Things were going along well. But the more she protested the more he became convinced that he was being lulled into therapeutic slumber. Finally, he indicated that she must choose between two alternatives: he could switch her to another analyst or she could go into a concomitant group experience. At this point, she began to ask about the nature of the group experience and how long it would be necessary. When she heard it was to be done on a trial basis for three months, all objections ceased.

When the group analyst interviewed her, he also found her a "Johnny-one-note," though admittedly the note he heard was a different one. She appeared to be suspicious about everything concerning the forthcoming experience: the appointment time during her lunch hour, the barrenness of his waiting room, the clutter on his desk, the fact that all the books on his shelves dealt with psychiatry, and the questions he asked about her past, parents, and dreams. Probing her skepticism, he found that she had doubts about his competence. She felt he was just putting on a good show to make it look as though he knew what he was doing. Her questioning attitude haunted the subsequent group sessions. She took everything he said to her with more than a grain of salt. She doubted the efficacy of group treatment and the value of anything a peer had to say.

During the initial group sessions she remained politely detached. One member observed that she seemed to be merely "putting in time." In a composed manner, she assured him this was a new experience for her and she was feeling her way into it.

But as her peers began to reach out to make contact with her, one member found her sweet; another, cautious; another, concerned; still another, haughty. Her attitude changed constantly, depending on which member addressed her. The group often complained it could find no single line to her personality. To the ten members, she seemed to be ten different people.

The only early mention she made of the group during her private sessions was that she found the members nagging and unpredictable. She blamed the group analyst, who she thought had no control over them or any sense of discipline. She had reservations about whether she could put up with the chaos for two more months.

One member became obsessively fascinated by her. He felt in her some kind of mystery that held the key to his difficulty in understanding women. He kept plying her with search questions: What did she do after work? How did she behave with her friends? Did she have any boy friends? What were her relations with her fellow employees? What was she really like on a consistent basis—"like if he lived with her"? Was she a tiger or a lady in bed? What was she like at breakfast? What would happen if she were not sweet to Mary, ironic to Jim, haughty to Susan, or cool to him?

In spite of her detached attitude toward the prying member, she found she could not brush off his insistent questioning. Nothing she could say diverted him. Sensing her growing withdrawal, the group analyst turned the group's attention to the pursuer. Why was he so interested in her?

At first, he was evasive. As the group pressed for reasons, members were surprised to find that she figured in his fantasies during the week. He could not get her out of his mind. From the moment she entered the group she had struck him as the spitting image of the impenetrable but

alluring mother of his childhood. He finally blurted out that
he loved her. The editor was appalled at this confession of
feeling, and told him flatly that he was "not her type." Nevertheless, she found herself both fascinated and frightened
by him.

Her individual sessions took a strange twist: How could
the analyst have been so callous as to put her in such a
compromising position? The analyst replied to her attack
with investigation: What was she trying to tell him? She
became shy and hesitant: Was he not aware of her feelings?
He wanted to know what feelings. She parried: How did he
think any man he could send her to could ever equal him?

The blandness dissipated. She revealed erotic fantasies
about him that had been hidden because of her fear of rejection. Once these positive feelings had a chance to emerge,
the reason for the unruffled surface became apparent: to
expose her feelings would have placed her in danger of
being rejected. When her feelings were accepted and understood, she relaxed a little and a variety of other emotions
began to edge into the open. With them came an interest in
her monotone responses to her group peers. When she
sought to explore her views of the members with them, the
ensuing interchanges would plunge her into a "cauldron of
confusion" and her composure would crumble. Only within
the sanctum of the individual session could she examine a
frozen front she presented to a particular member. The
analyst would help her probe for the anxiety and the feared
fantasy behind it. Once she understood each "front" a rich
complex of feelings would take its place. The group members praised and reinforced the emerging personal changes.

Between the members and individual analyst the gene-
sis of these many "faces of Eve" was pieced together. The
patient had been shifted as a child from one relative to
another because of recurrent squabbles or break-ups between her parents. If her presence became inconvenient for
one set of temporary foster parents, she was dumped on
other relatives. The only rationale she was able to work out
was that she was the cause for each shift: it was due to some
activity, attitude, or behavior on her part. After much trial
and error she learned to play a careful role with each of the
people around her in order to hide her true feelings of
anger, jealousy, fear, or warmth. Whatever each person she

needed at the moment wanted or responded to was what she specialized in. Behind this pattern was an earlier one: a feeling that somehow she was responsible for the parental break-ups.

In the group she became quite spontaneous and supportive and was regarded by many as its most valuable member—a position which she relished.

The last hurdle for her was the group analyst, whom she regarded with unswerving mistrust and considered inept. She continuously corrected his speech and usage, and many times she hinted at his "low origins." She suggested that he dressed like a clown; instead of clothes, he wore costumes. These critiques were low-keyed, and she retracted them if another member objected.

What baffled her was the admiration and loyalty the other members displayed toward him. They would often defend or warmly praise him. Discussing this with her individual analyst, she insisted that somehow the group leader must be seducing these people.

One session she began, as usual, to point out the group analyst's flaws. Instead of accepting her barbs passively, he asked other members what they thought of her comments, selecting members who at the time were in a negative frame of mind toward him. When supported by these peers, she expanded on her fault-finding, and a mass of malevolent material poured out against people who mislead others. Some members admired how she put things so well into words and others agreed that the analyst made many "boo-boos." The editor then began to feel more charitable toward him. At the same time, she began to look at her own attitude in a more rational manner. Though the critical pattern continued, she began to wonder if it were not a bit extreme.

In the midst of another of her evaluations of him as ill-trained, clumsy, and flippant, one of the members, a social worker, asked her if she knew the group analyst's record. She said she did not need to know, his behavior was enough for her. But at the following session she began to ask about him. She was startled to learn that he had gone to Yale, taught at universities and institutes, and written papers on the treatment of groups.

She spent several individual sessions trying to sort out this information. Why was she so critical of him? Why did she regard him with contempt and mistrust? The facts and her feelings did not jibe.

Each of her attempts to explore the matter with the group analyst directly was done in a provocative way. She would end up feeling misunderstood and disbelieving everything her fellow members said.

While grappling with this predicament in an individual session, she had an association which started to unravel the tangled threads. A picture came to mind. The family was sitting around the kitchen table after dinner. Her father took out his weekly pay and laid it on the table. Her mother compared the sum with an annotated list of what was needed for family survival that week. The pay was inadequate. Her mother broke into tears.

Her father reacted with fury. He told her that he was not a magician. He was doing the best he could do, and if she thought she could do better, good luck to her. With that, he stormed out.

Her mother counted the money over and over again as the children watched. Then she suddenly went to the phone and called the wife of a neighbor who worked with the father and asked how much the neighbor's husband brought home from the job. It was more by a third than the amount the patient's father had put on the table.

The jig-saw pieces of ineptness and distrust began to fit together. She saw the group analyst as the father of her early years. She culled from her memory one incident after another to support these characteristics on a more personal level of broken promises, misleading information, and emotional statements which were not borne out in reality. While the group therapist had been the unreliable father, the individual analyst had been the reliable parent she had never had. Once she grasped the roots of her attitude, her need for the defensive mistrust evaporated. The fear was gone. She started treating the group analyst as a friendly person.

Meanwhile, her whole way of relating to the world underwent a metamorphosis. She found herself approaching new relationships with a minimum of apprehension. There was little need to display only one side of her personality to each person. No longer could she be labeled as bland, negative, suspicious, cool, or sweet. Her responses were close to the ones that were appropriate to the moment. The need for protective ego compartmentalization was cast off. A complex and multi-faceted personality took its place.

The concept of multiplicity in settings, transference, interpretation, and resolution provides a clear rationale and justification for conjoint analysis. Working conjointly, we help the members of our groups and each other compare and effectively confront the ways the patient operates, the roles he plays, and the attitudes he takes to protect himself. To do this, we make generous use of our induced feelings, which at times we share with each other, to dissolve defenses and unravel interpersonal enigmas that so many patients present today.

*Chapter 3*

# LIMITATIONS AND CONTRAINDICATIONS OF CONJOINT TREATMENT

## LIMITATIONS

What is the case against conjoint treatment? To begin with, there is tradition. Many analysts tend to deny the existence of induced resistances. There are analytic difficulties that are caused by the personality of the professional. Bibring-Lehner[1] pointed out that the difficulties her patient had experienced with his first analyst were caused by the similarity between the behavior of the latter and his father. As far as many orthodox analysts are concerned, any problem with the patient is either a transferential resistance he has overlooked or a countertransference reaction to which he is oblivious and cannot deal with because of some kink in himself he has not worked out.

Though it is often denied, the limitations of personality are always there. Some analysts can deal with any syndrome except addiction. Others cannot tolerate the rituals of the obsessive. Still others are clay in the unconscious hands of the psychopath.

Supervision, careful countertransference controls, even a return to a training analysis may not make a noticeable dent in these practitioners' ability to deal with patients that they find antithetical to their innate attitudes, morals, or character patterns.

On the group treatment side, the reservations about conjoint treatment are amply expressed by Slavson,[8] who recommended that the individual therapist and group therapist should be the same.

Bach[1] later supported this view of the negative effects of "parallel treatment." Bach even opposed any individual consultation. He felt that it fired the "neurotic contact operations involving the analyst." It merely reinforced the patient's position that the only figure that mattered in the group was the therapist. Bach felt that it intensified any dependency feelings, and that this had a detrimental effect on the interactions between the patient and his peers in the shared setting. Bach did agree that where therapists keep in sporadic contact with each other, patients can gain from conjoint treatment.

Schwartz and Wolf[7] feel that even when the collaboration of two therapists is at its best, it presents all the problems one finds in combined therapy. These problems are mainly those centering on dependency.

Practice indicates that there are significant limitations to conjoint treatment. The group analyst must forego any aspirations toward being a psychological archeologist. His province is essentially the "now." Fantasies, historical incidents, determining traumas of formative years, and the rich world of dreams cannot be leisurely or meticulously explored. He has to be content with bits and pieces of the intimate details of his members' worlds. He has to restrain any interest in their unconscious lives. The best he can do is to extrapolate and reconstruct the past from the present. The tracing of transference resistances to their sources can be done only as the flow of communication permits. To do otherwise, investigating with individual members, stops the group resistances from unfolding naturally, and what ensues is a dyadic session within the group setting. Therefore, in the group analyst's thinking, constellation is just as important as constitution. Thus, the present interpersonal conflicts receive greater attention than childhood entanglements, perhaps because he feels he can do something about them.

The group analyst's true forte is ego analysis. He is in an optimal position to study, examine, and resolve all obstacles to emotional verbal communication between the members. While his individual colleague is privy to the arcane alleyways of his members' thinking and feeling patterns, the group analyst has to content himself with becoming master at modifying their defensive systems.

> An individual analyst made a decision to cut back on his practice in order to open up his Friday afternoons for leisure activity. He sent four patients who saw him during that time to group therapy. They now saw him twice a week and had one group session with another therapist.
>
> The latter practitioner conducted his groups in a conscientious, vigorous manner, and saw all his group people individually. He took an active interest in the new arrivals and felt he needed a complete picture of them. The group sessions turned into an exploration and ventilation of the problems, dreams, anecdotal experiences, and biographical material of the newcomers. He either focused on them individually or mobilized the rest of the members to investigate them.
>
> But the veteran group members could not see any reason to excavate all this material. They had business of their own. The group therapist dealt with their dissatisfactions in their individual sessions with him. He explained that the process was the best way to educate less sophisticated members and incorporate them into the group process.
>
> During the individual sessions, each of the new members complained to the referring analyst that there seemed to be one patient and a bevy of junior analysts at work in

every group session, and he or she was the patient. As a subgroup, they saw no reason to "bare their souls" in public when they could do the same in the individual sessions.

In telephone conversations with the group therapist it became apparent that he was a "driven delver." He had to know everything. He defended his concern to uncover all the "relevant data" about the novitiates—he was not comfortable with "ignorance" and could not interpret unless he knew what was going on inside his patients.

Eventually, all four referrals found acceptable rationales for dropping the group experience. If the analyst had merely fixed his attention on the working surface, studying the interchanges among all the members, the experience would have been fruitful for all concerned and a treatment-destructive resistance would not have developed and been acted out.

### Attitudes toward the Individual and Group Analysts

Another type of limitation is of a more serious nature. In conjoint treatment, there is frequently a tendency for patients to develop a positive relation to their individual analyst first and a negative or ambivalent attitude to their group analyst. In other words, the individual analyst resolves their resistances to the verbal expression of their hostile feelings, but the actual release tends to be triggered off in the group setting.[5] Something quite picayune may cause a sudden release of aggression, often directed at the group analyst. Not only that, but if there should be smoldering negative attitudes in the other members, the release of uncomfortable feelings will ignite these into flame. An enormous amount of conscious and unconscious aggression may be directed at the group leader. This factor has far-reaching implications for the character structure and training of the group analyst. His insulation barrier has to be strengthened. He must be capable of receiving and accepting unpleasant feelings abruptly and sometimes without warning.

In a clinical setting, a therapist worked for six months with a 30-year-old borderline patient. He had come for treatment sporadically over the years, dropping out on one pretext or another, usually because of the lack of the ten dollar fee. This was part of his life's pattern. He would begin on many paths, only to halt each journey when the going got rough. He claimed he had little energy and attributed it to his inability to "get a good night's sleep." When he was not working, he spent his hours at a movie or in the public library.

In a supervisory conference it was decided that there were two major difficulties: his loneliness and his denied aggression. It was felt that he could benefit from the social stimulation offered by the group experience. Accordingly, he was placed in an ongoing group at the clinic which consisted of an admixture of hysterical and depressive patients. The expectations about the group's ability to socialize him were not realized. He remained withdrawn and quiet. Because of his inoffensiveness and his tendency to blend into the group feeling, he escaped most confrontations. Members just ignored him.

Nevertheless, he reported in his individual sessions that he found the group stimulating. He appeared to gain understanding of himself through partial identification with the members. He would observe, imitate, and sometimes correct his behavior in his everyday life, using various members as models.

Meanwhile, the individual therapist worked well and skillfully with him to resolve his objections toward experiencing his negative feelings. This work consisted of giving him a minimum of verbal feeding. When his frustration-aggression became too high for him, the analyst would ask one or two questions about matters which had nothing to do with him personally, such as "What was the name of the movie?" or "What kind of fish did the restaurant serve?" In time the patient became more tolerant of the lack of feeding and could let himself experience some of his less positive feelings. Admittedly, this was not a giant step, but it freed him enough so that he could report he had stood up to some "razzing" by his fellow workers at his job as a shipping clerk.

As the patient was beginning to feel his identity, his group peers' difficulties with their own anger were beginning to peak. The depressives complained a little more about their sad lot or would drift off into sleep. The hysterical members' lateness and absences increased. They had more colds, cramps, skin eruptions.

Bringing these defensive operations to their attention was not of much avail. So the group analyst began to focus on a consistent confrontation of one pattern: the way they ignored the late arrival of a few members. Some members started to become restive under the "nagging," particularly the borderline patient, who wanted the analyst "to lay off." When the analyst persisted, members brought into play other defenses. They either ignored his presence or acted as if he had not spoken, picking up their litany at the point where the analyst had interrupted it to point out a tardiness.

Just before the group's meeting time, the analyst usually attended a staff meeting where cases were presented or invited speakers were asked to address the therapists. One of the speakers, a prominent theoretician, ran over his time, and out of deference and respect he was not interrupted. The group analyst arrived at the group session ten minutes late.

All the members were assembled. His entry was greeted with a simmering silence. As if nothing had happened, one member picked up what he had been saying to another member. The borderline patient broke in with a lacerating lecture on the subject of analysts who hypocritically tell others "to do what they say, not what they do." The intensity of the assault startled the others, but it also energized them. The depressive patients seized the opportunity to unburden themselves of long suppressed grievances: the analyst was a masked martinet more interested in the schedule than in the members. The hysterics joined the chorus with more raucous remonstrations, though their comments were more pointed. They had detailed examples of his aberrations, large and small, and delineated them with painful accuracy. Any emotional lull in the attack was refueled by the borderline patient's vehemence. With uncanny accuracy, he would take the presented material just as it passed its emotional peak and charge it anew.

The onslaught on the group analyst was devastating. He

experienced both their conscious accusations and their un-conscious transferential rage. He turned their arguments against himself. This led to a paralyzing anxiety state which alternated with a defensive explanatory stance when the members demanded that he answer them. Soon they were all yelling at the top of their voices, each escalating the others' fury. Led by the borderline patient, they all agreed they had had enough of his incompetence. As a group, they got up and walked out. To the analyst it looked like the end of the group and the nadir of his professional life.

Fortunately, several experienced supervisors, present in the clinic, were attracted by the tumult, and they at once convened with him. After he told his tale, the group's dynamics were explained to him. His countertransference was analyzed, his defense was supported, and his insulation barrier was strengthened. What to do with the group technically was carefully spelled out to him.

That night he called each member and asked him or her to come in to see him for a few minutes individually. Much to his surprise, each agreed. During these short sessions, he explored each member's impression of the meeting. Then he encouraged each member to talk about his or her further thoughts and feelings at the next session.

Everyone arrived on time for the following group session. Though the attack was subdued, a residue of rage was expressed. The analyst made sure that each member spoke his piece. At the end of the meeting he congratulated the group. They had the right feelings if this was the way they saw the analyst's behavior and, what was more, they had communicated them effectively and openly. They would have to talk more on the subject.

The group experienced itself as a cohesive unit. The members left feeling elated, particularly the borderline patient, who had achieved a new position in the eyes of the others.

In the following individual session, he was reflective. He had been shocked by his own outburst initially and then awed by his doggedness. He spoke in wonderment about sleeping soundly the night of the "walk-out" and about the enormous energy he experienced the next day. A thought had been percolating in his mind all week: perhaps he could go back to night school and stick with it until he finished his education.

What was of import here, was that the obstacles to the discharge of destructive feelings had been worked through in individual sessions, but the release came in the group session. The release triggered off a general response. The group resistance against the communication of aggressive thoughts would still have to be worked on before it was resolved, though a giant step had been taken.

The group analyst has to be on the alert to see that too much aggression is not mobilized nor released at any one time. He has to work for a balance between frustration and gratification to keep the release of hostility at a low steady level.

If the conjoint analysts had been a more seasoned pair, and each had understood how the other worked, the outburst might have been more controlled or measured. But many conjoint workers never get this far. Many steer the talk away from any open rage. They fear the aggression of their disturbed patients and devote their efforts to resolving resistances to sexual or positive feelings. But it has been often observed that a negative, even intense confrontation with the group analyst early in the members' experience forms and solidifies peer cohesiveness and maintains an atmosphere of interpersonal accessibility among the participants.

## CONTRAINDICATIONS

For many preoedipal personalities, combined analysis may not be the treatment of choice. Severely deprived personalities, whose maturational needs are extreme and demanding, may not find any group situation salutary or beneficial. And the other members of a group may experience these patients as burdensome or abrasive. For example, a patient with deep unrelenting despondency will not only drag down the emotional tonality of a group or slow its therapeutic pace, but will also view the experience of being among others as an "ordeal."

A 22-year-old severely depressed garment worker was seen individually for seven months in a clinical setting. In spite of the objections of the therapist, who felt that she was in a "regressed state" and needed "mirroring and joining tailored to her special communications," it was the opinion of the supervisor that the depression was of a defensive nature, and was a thin veneer over aggression. A unilateral decision was made to place her in an on-going group.

Obedient and compliant, she entered the group without a complaint. The members, a lively crew who had worked together for over two years, were apt to express their irritation in good-humored but sharp barbs that had a penetrating effect. It took them only three sessions to evaluate the new member accurately: she was an "albatross around their necks." They dealt with her by not addressing themselves to her at all. Instead, when they felt any aggression toward the analyst, they attacked him for putting a "blob" in the group.[3]

The patient complained in individual sessions that the treatment she was receiving in the group was humiliating. As far as her therapist was concerned, she was correct. Nevertheless, he carried out his supervisor's instructions and sought to analyze her resistance to talking about the mortification of being ignored by the group. No matter from what angle he approached the subject with her, he could make no progress. Her aggression was not ready to work its way to the surface. Other personal problems were more pressing. She repeatedly told him that she was going to stop going to the group sessions, and eventually she did just that. The only reason she gave was that "it was a waste of time." She never returned to a group experience, though she did make some therapeutic progress over the next year.

The premature admission of the patient to the group may have been a factor here. But what was more to the point was that a group experience was not indicated in terms of her difficulties. The group did not provide the appropriate emotional climate that the individual therapist was capable of giving. The supervisor, who was partial to the group as a therapeutic tool, had imposed his assessment on the student therapist.

## Apprehensive Patients

Conjoint analysis is frequently contraindicated with continuous and pervasive states of apprehension.[9] Patients of this type can monopolize group time and absorb the members' energies. Once their peers rise up in revolt against this use of them, the patient may leave each meeting more upset than he entered it.

> A 30-year-old writer of children's books was anxious about everything: work, subways, neighbors, heights, dogs. As she put it, "You can't name anything I'm not scared of." In spite of her extreme phobic attitude, she was a person of redoubtable courage. By restricting her contacts with the outside world, she had managed to make a name for herself in her work. Most of her business was conducted by phone. At one point in her therapy she became interested in a self-help course which instructed her to "overcome fear by doing what one fears most." This was something that she had been doing with limited success most of her life anyway, but, fired by this passage, she announced to her therapist that she was going to confront her fear of people by entering a therapy group. He agreed that there were times when confronting one's apprehensions could be helpful.[19] The only reservations he had was her readiness to take this step. She did not want to discuss the pros and cons of this decision. She was tired of sitting around commiserating with herself.
>
> Through a recommendation made by her publisher, she found her own group analyst. Her individual therapist knew him and was apprised of her progress in the group.
>
> First, she forced herself to go to the group sessions. Once there, she felt great anxiety about talking in the group. Each obstacle she overcame more by force of will than by understanding.
>
> The turning point came when she summoned up enough courage to start describing her daily anxieties. Each

week she would detail a list of the major ones. Initially, the members were helpful to her by forcing her to focus on the here-and-now fears, but invariably she would return to her list. Then they started to understand each fear separately. As soon as one was laid to rest, she would spring up with another one. These apprehensions took precedence over any interactions with the members. Frequently, she would interrupt what was going on to describe an anxiety that had slipped into her mind because of something a member had mentioned in passing. Soon she was the object of exasperated outbursts which would silence her. After the session, she would corner the group analyst for some supportive statements. If these were not forthcoming, she would leave the office more agitated than when she arrived. She found she could not sleep at night, could no longer force herself to work, and her paralysis was more severe than ever.

She dropped out of the group. In her individual sessions she looked back on the experience as a nightmare. The only thing she thought she had gained from it was the conviction that willpower did not provide a solution.

## Other Patients

Conjoint treatment has limitations for other types of patients. A mind which is cluttered with introjected partial objects and cannot seem to find a central cohesive line for itself may experience the group setting as just another chaotic calamity. Patients still grappling with fantasies that fragment reality have difficulty following the interchanges of their peers. The individual therapist then finds himself relegated to the onerous task of clearing away the psychological underbrush that has sprung up after each group session has reactivated the partial objects. Patients caught in delusionary states, whether visual or auditory, may be so out of touch with their environment that they will frighten or infuriate other group members. If they are to be placed in a group, they need a special setting. The individual therapist has to limit the communications to reality subjects or object-oriented topics.

These are only a few of the people who must have a lengthy unspecified period of one-to-one work before they can tolerate the suggestion that they might benefit from exchanges with other fellow human beings.

## RELATIONSHIP BETWEEN THE THERAPISTS

One obvious drawback of conjoint work for the individual analyst is that it cannot take the place of the systematic development that occurs when a patient is seen daily under set conditions. The individual analyst may find he has to fill in gaps in the unfolding pathology because in the group setting the patient has dealt with some critical matter which he has only touched on in the private sessions.

The transference often takes unforeseen twists and turns because of the patient's contacts with his peers or the group analyst. Many a private session is taken up with a group matter, interrupting a theme that has just begun to emerge between the patient and the individual analyst, or the patient and his significant history.

This unpredictability is exasperating to many seasoned professionals who find the patient's inner instability enough to deal with without having to cope with compounding external stimulants or "unnecessary static." Many analysts advocate jealously safeguarding the transference and avoiding contamination. Greenacre[4] suggests we ought to pay more attention to splitting of the transference and many analysts have agreed with her.

> A highly respected individual analyst was faced with a dilemma. He made it a practice to see his patients at least four times a week, preferably five. One of them, a 40-year-old stockbroker who had been with him for 18 months, had declared that he was a member of a "depressed industry" and could no longer afford the weekly fee. But the patient did not want to break off treatment at this juncture of his analysis.

After much discussion, the patient came up with a temporary solution. His wife had been attending a group for over a year and was enthusiastic about the results. She had urged him to do the same, particularly since the group fee was only a third as much as he paid for individual sessions. It had occurred to the patient that he might manage his finances if he saw his individual analyst twice a week and spent one session in a group.

Reluctantly, the analyst agreed. The patient at once interviewed his wife's group analyst and was accepted into treatment with him.

From the start of this makeshift arrangement, the individual analyst found himself fretful. The analysis had taken on a new texture. It appeared to him that the transference had been muddied; the patient had overnight adopted a new set of relatives with whom he had to grapple; the session following his group meeting was either "choppy" or tangential to what they had been developing in their previous session; there was an inordinate concern with reality problems; and a regression at the service of the ego had dwindled.

The more the patient intruded his group experiences into the private sessions, the more vexed the analyst became. He began to doubt the efficacy of this arrangement. A few discrete inquiries about the group analyst revealed that he was not orthodoxically trained. His school of thought was an admixture of the Freudian, Neo-Freudian, Sullivanian, and other innovative approaches. The individual analyst began to hint to the patient that he was unable to follow what was going on in him since they had embarked on this new course. He was honest about it because he could not see any connection between what occurred in the group and what happened between the patient and himself. Soon he was actively viewing the group as a resistance to treatment, and he approached the patient's communications with this in mind.

The patient got the message and both agreed that a vacation was in order. The overt reason was a deteriorating financial situation. The patient dropped his individual analyst and remained in the group. He later returned to individual treatment with an experienced conjoint analyst and successfully completed his treatment.

The respected individual analyst never contacted the group analyst. When the group analyst called him the individual analyst would listen politely and interject an occasional "I see ..." but there was never the sense of two professionals working together. Most of the individual analyst's views were communicated to the group analyst through the patient, either directly or indirectly.

Any time one form of analysis is considered superior to or more effective than the other, the professionals cannot be considered to be working conjointly. For one thing, the patient misses all the potential benefits of this modality of treatment. For another, the patient knows the preferences of his therapists and can exploit them in the service of his transferential machinations. Finally, the therapists sooner or later drift apart and the working relationship either ruptures or dissolves imperceptibly.

Patients referred to a particular analyst invariably did well for about a year. Then an inexplicable pattern would set in. Each patient would begin to observe that he had gotten as much as he could out of the group. Within a month or so he would take his leave for excellent reasons, often having nothing directly to do with the treatment, but would manage to continue in individual analysis.

The professionals concerned, met several times for postmortem evaluations over lunch. These meetings were warm and open. The possibilities in the patient's dynamics were explored and reexamined. The conclusions they arrived at seemed sound and logical at the moment. But the group analyst found that he left with several gnawing questions. Why did the patients not stop both treatments simultaneously? Why was there the high number of early terminations with this analyst compared to his conjoint work with other professionals?

During a group session, one of these terminating patients repeated a remark made by his individual analyst, to the effect that "it is time to test your new strengths in the real world." When members brought to his attention the fact that he still demonstrated difficulties in the group and asked why he could not do both, he replied, "This isn't life. At best, it is a laboratory."

The group analyst decided it was time for another lunch. This time the subject was not the patient, it was the individual analyst's basic assumptions about their work together. After some evasion the differences surfaced.

The individual therapist saw the group as a parameter, effective and beneficial up to a point, but to be discarded when a firm transference was established and an infantile neurosis was in full swing. When the chips were down, he considered individual work by far the more critical of the two therapeutic instruments. In his thinking, there was only one true therapy and it took place in the dyadic setting.

Conjoint treatment stands or falls on the relationship between the two therapists.[6] If there is a misunderstanding, which can be intricate and often obscure, between the professionals involved, the effect may not be apparent for some time.

An individual analyst, who had worked conjointly for years, referred to a group a patient with whom he did not seem to be making progress. His colleague sensed that the patient had been "overfed" and gave no interpretations whatsoever to him. When he paid him any individual attention, he would do it indirectly, asking the other members why the patient was not talking about his feelings toward them. Unwittingly, the two analysts were looking at the same person from diametrically opposed positions.

As the patient developed more aggression toward the group analyst, the individual analyst found that he was "opening up." Each time the patient complained about an incident in group, the analyst found himself querying him with "What did the group therapist tell you about that?" The patient would reply, "Nothing." "Did you ask him?" The patient picked up the idea that he was not getting enough attention and began to press the group analyst for insights.

When his requests were met with more investigation, he complained to the individual analyst that the group was an interesting experience but he was "lost in the crowd and ignored." This was not investigated, though several times the patient questioned the advisability of continuing in the group.

In their infrequent contacts the professionals made no mention of untoward developments. The group analyst had no idea that a treatment-destructive resistance was developing. As far as he could tell, the patient was participating in the shared interchanges with his peers. But the resistance solidified when the patient began to see the group leader as his passive father, who had little direct influence in the household. This was not dealt with in either setting. In the group, the patient did not mention it. In the private sessions the analyst did not focus on it, though he had heard that the patient had left home rather than rebel openly against his ineffectual father. The end result was that the patient made a decision to drop the group. By this time it was difficult to deal with the resistance.

Only after the break was made did the analysts confront the fact that they had been working at cross-purposes. The individual analyst had developed a countertransference to his patient which had led to much feeding of information and blunted his usual perceptiveness. The group analyst had made the technical error of assuming that much of what he observed was being taken care of in the individual session.

It is of critical importance that both workers agree, either tacitly or explicitly on a treatment plan. Otherwise, resistances will develop that will be overlooked.

With experience and time it becomes unnecessary to discuss every development of each patient. Each conjoint team works differently. One team would have a systematic review of each patient they were treating. This was done over the telephone about once every three months. Another team made it a point to keep in close touch on all borderline and schizoid patients. The members of one team contacted each other only to communicate a warning about what a patient was planning to do which might be deleterious to the treatment process. Many teams never discuss the people they are dealing with unless some crisis or unyielding resistance appears.

The authors consult on all our patients, but not necessarily about the dynamics of each one. We tend to talk about the "line of continuity"—how a theme is being played out in both settings. Our most effective work has been accomplished when each of us has had an intuitive grasp of what the other is doing. Our "third ears" tend to be in touch not only with the patients, but also with each other through them. Through the years of working together, we have developed the knack of sensing the meaning of what is taking place before us and relating it to what is happening in the other setting. While one of us analyzes a resistance, the other may reinforce it. While one of us symbolically gratifies libidinal needs, the other may frustrate them. We always work for a careful balance between the two polarities. The defenses and buried wishes may better be activated in one setting and strengthened or resolved in the other.

Some patients like to know that the analysts constantly consult each other about them. Then they feel as if they have two parents who are sharing a mutual concern for their well-being. They are not above testing one or the other analyst to see if some piece of critical knowledge was communicated to him by his colleagues.

In contradistinction, a number of patients like the separation and wish that the analysts would never talk to each other. They crave the confidentiality of the individual session. Because these people will sooner or later know if their confidence has been betrayed, it is foolhardy and pointless to divulge to a fellow colleague any information they reveal until the resistance is resolved, and it can prove quite a formidable one. Other patients do not seem to care either way. In practice, it is a wise policy to explore with all patients, at suitable junctures, how they feel about the analysts sharing the material that the patient has revealed.

# Chapter 4

# THE PATIENT IN INDIVIDUAL TREATMENT

In this chapter we wish to explicate our orientation to the treatment of the individual in one-to-one treatment both conceptually and through clinical examples. As was stated in Chapter 1, our view of the patient is anchored to Freud's metapsychological view of man and supplemented by concepts derived from Hartmann, Erikson, and others.[1, 7, 10]

## THE FIRST INTERVIEW

When the candidate for psychotherapy or psychoanalysis applies for assistance, he is either tacitly or overtly acknowledging that some aspects of either his internal life and/or his interpersonal relationships are not the way he would like them to be. Very often he is suffering from symptoms like phobias, compulsions, or psychosomatic complaints; more frequently, he is dissatisfied with his relationships with others such as in a marriage or work. Almost always, the prospective patient dislikes aspects of his own self and the way he appears to himself.

It has been our experience that most prospective patients, particularly in a first interview, appreciate a quiet but interested listener who encourages the individual to complain about what and who ails him or her. As the prospective patient elaborates on his symptom picture and other distressful aspects of his life, he frequently is then enabled to discuss, and often spontaneously, salient aspects of his life history: relationships with parents, siblings, peers, teachers, etc.

In the discussion of his history, most candidates for psychoanalytic treatment usually refer to how and when "significant others" betrayed, hurt, or angered them. Often, the therapist in the first interview can begin to get a glimpse of how the patient's maturational needs were not met. He may learn for example that the patient was not given sufficient freedom to love, or to express anger; to have autonomy and independence at appropriate times; to enjoy his sexual impulses, etc. While it is important for the analyst *not* to interpret or make verbal judgments prematurely, he silently begins to think of the kind of therapeutic relationship and therapeutic experiences that the patient will need from him.

The first interview, in addition to helping the patient reveal whatever he can about his psychological and interpersonal problems and his history, should also afford him the opportunity to express his fantasies on how he would like to experience himself eventually and how he fantasizes what the therapist will do in treatment.

In our view many therapists err in the first interview by puncturing the patient's fantasies. Instead of telling the patient that neither he, the therapist, nor he, the patient, will emerge into a God, Superman, or Superwoman, it is important to give the patient an ear on what the latter would like for himself. It becomes grist for the future therapeutic mill. Often, prospective patients "drop-out" of treatment prematurely because the therapist interprets them away or subtly demonstrates his disapproval of what the patient wants for himself instead of listening to his fantasies, wishes, and complaints.

Sooner or later, every patient eventually brings his self-destructive patterns into the transference relationship. We have often found that in the first interview it is sometimes helpful to ask the man or woman who leaves relationships when angry, when does he think this will occur in the current treatment relationship. Likewise, we suggest that when unpaid bills, latenesses to appointments, and other self-destructive behavior occurs with the therapist, as it probably will, it will be helpful to investigate the meaning of this in future psychotherapeutic sessions.

During the first interview, part of the patient's modus vivendi that will be exhibited is the way he resists progressive communication.[10] He may avoid the past or the present, squelch aggressive or sexual feelings, comply or be passively or overtly aggressive, ingratiate himself or avoid the therapist. While these patterns are not usually discussed in the first interview, they are clues to the therapist as to how the transference neurosis will evolve.

It is usually suggested to the patient that treatment for the first few months will be on a trial basis so that both parties can determine if they can work reasonably well with each other. Although individual treatment can be anywhere from one to five times a week, our own experience has been to start on a once or twice a week basis and increase the frequency later, if the need occurs.

## THE HONEYMOON PERIOD

After several interviews at which the patient can further elucidate on his symptom picture, he is asked to take the couch and free associate. Most patients usually do not have difficulty taking the couch, but some do. When the patient protests, he is not forced or cajoled but instead, he is invited to look at his fears.

The patient's fear of the couch is frequently a fear of passive and helpless feelings. The patient thinks that he will be reduced to a crying baby, because he both unconsciously wishes this role but is concomitantly humiliated by it. Due to the anxiety that emanates from his helpless feelings the patient may say that he does not want "to be in a submissive or subordinate position." Here, it is important to ask and analyze with the patient. "What bothers him about feeling submissive, helpless, etc.?" A great deal of therapeutic progress can take place when the patient is afforded the opportunity of "sitting up" and discussing his fears and forbidden wishes about passivity, submissiveness, and regression, which are at the root of his "couch phobia."

For many patients the initial period of treatment can be termed "The Honeymoon Period."[2] The opportunity to freely discuss feelings, thoughts, and memories with an attentive but nonintrusive listener usually induces in the patient a feeling that what he says and therefore, who he is, is important. Pent up and somewhat forbidden impulses that are not censured by the therapist enhances self-esteem and frees parts of the ego to then examine more disturbing conflicts later.

In order for deeper conflicts to emerge in the transference relationship with the therapist, we have found that during the first few months of one-to-one treatment, the therapist should remain quite passive, using himself essentially to help the patient communicate his problems and the story of his life as freely as possible.

## RESISTANCES

The increased self-esteem together with the initial positive transference or working alliance usually aids the patient in taking further risks in self-revelation.[5] He may risk making demands on the therapist or risk criticizing him; he may risk the expression of his ambivalence about forbidden sexual or aggressive fantasies or experiences; or, he may take the chance of sharing with the analyst embarrassing or traumatic incidents from the story of his life.[11]

As the patient attempts to explore his conflicts in more depth, the treatment situation becomes somewhat less comfortable. Certain hopes or wishes that the patient thought the therapist would gratify are not being gratified. For example, the patient may have wanted to emerge as the therapist's special and lovable child and instead he is just understood. The patient may have expected that the therapist would agree with him and take his side in a marital or job dispute and instead the therapist just continues to try to understand the patient's ambivalence. Or, the patient may seek forgiveness for past misdeeds and the therapist's behavior is again experienced as frustrating by the patient because again, the analyst will not forgive but try to help the patient look at the wishes and fantasies that propelled "the misdeeds."

After the honeymoon period, then, the patient begins to manifest various forms of resistances, i.e., id, ego, superego, or transference resistances. Although it is not always predictable, what we have found is that certain id resistances appear on the scene first. By an id resistance, we are referring to immature or infantile cravings which the patient is still seeking to gratify but which are inappropriate in the present.

> Alice, aged 30, during her twelfth session took the couch and began to hit the wall with her fist. When the therapist told her that it would be best for her treatment to put her feelings into words and not hit the wall she bellowed: "You're a balding bastard who gives me next to nothing!" (Silence of a minute) "See, you give me nothing. I pay you a damn good fee, tell you what's on my mind and all you do is sit there." When Alice was asked what she wanted from

the therapist, she replied, "You are supposed to know. You never anticipate what I want. I'm supposed to ask you what I want. You never freely and spontaneously give of yourself. Come on, give me what I want!" Here, the therapist said that he did not know what she wanted unless he was helped to know by her.

Alice then gave a picture of how she always wanted and expected indulgences from boy friends, bosses, group therapy colleagues and how nobody ever took over. She wanted so much to be mothered and everybody rejected her. In later sessions she recalled how she had hated her mother for not being more available and with some insight could say, "I guess my demanding behavior can turn some people off."

When requests of the analyst by the patient are clearly identified as id resistances, it is important for the therapy that the wishes *not* be gratified. As the patient is helped to put into words what he or she wants, several therapeutic gains can take place. First, the patient is helped to assume a more adult role by requesting rather than demanding, ego functions get stronger as the patient masters and controls impulses rather than the latter mastering him, and finally, as impulses, wishes, and fantasies are fully expressed, their infantile quality becomes exposed and eventually relinquished.

Ego resistances are the most universal and predominant in therapy. The ego, as we recall, attempts to ward off instincts, superego commands, and threats from the environment.

Bob, aged 36, at his twenty-fifth session arrived with a headache. He couldn't understand why he had a headache because "everything is going so well." He remarked that the therapist was kind and understanding so he knew "it couldn't be the therapy." However, Bob reported a dream in which he was walking down Broadway (the route he takes to the analyst's office) and someone from "behind" (the patient was on the couch with the analyst behind him) hit him over the head.

As the patient associated to being hit from behind, he recalled how he is always on guard everywhere so that this will not happen. He then with anger said, "Nobody can be trusted. They are all trying to put you down. My wife does that, my boss does that, and you know (silence of thirty seconds) you probably feel like a big shot while I'm down here on the couch! Gee, my headache is disappearing!"

Bob was defending himself against the aggression that he felt toward the analyst. A competitive man who had to be in a superior position, his headache was a somatic expression of his anger toward the therapist. As Bob could feel his anger, he did not need his compliant defense so much. Of course, his anger, which was analyzed eventually, was his expression of contempt for not being able to be the omnipotent baby that he was always trying so hard to be.

 Superego resistances are formed by the patient to ward off ideas, feelings, or memories for which he believes he should be punished or censored. Because the analytic situation stimulates the arousal of repressed and unacceptable feelings, superego resistances are also quite ubiquitous.

Carol, in her thirty-second session, took the couch and after a silence of three minutes said, "I'm a terrible person!" (Silence of thirty seconds) "I hear you treat competent and capable people; I'm worthless and a jerk. I'm sexually unresponsive, nasty to my husband, provocative with men in general, and a no-goodnik in general." When there were repeated statements by Carol that she was an awful person who should not be tolerated by anybody, the analyst remarked, "I think you are trying awfully hard to get me to hate you and throw you out."

The patient cried intensely and then went on to express several oral fantasies: sucking on the analyst's penis, eating a breast, swallowing the analyst, etc. She talked about how she had always wanted close contact with a person (really a symbiosis), but was afraid she would eat the person up or be eaten. Her strong oral aggression was being defended by equally as powerful superego admonitions.

It is important to recognize that when the patient brings out a great deal of self-hate, he should not be reassured that he is an "O.K. person." Rather, the impulses which feed the masochistic defense will emerge if the therapist goes along with the patient's superego resistances.[8, 10, 11] When Carol was told that she was provocatively trying to get the analyst to beat her up and throw her out, her own sadistic fantasies could emerge and then, and only then, could her superego controls be somewhat diminished.

By a transference resistance, we mean that operation by the patient which deflects ideas, feelings, or fantasies towards the analyst because they are too painful or anxiety provoking to the patient. Inasmuch as we contend that transference reactions, the transference neurosis and their analyses constitutes the heart of therapy, we are very much interested in helping the patient resolve his transference resistances. As the patient experiences in the treatment his myriad reactions to the analyst, he is unfolding his neurotic and maladaptive conflicts, i.e., his id, ego, and superego resistances. One of the most common transference resistances is projecting on to the therapist, the patient's own unacceptable thoughts and wishes.

Donald, a 40-year-old salesman, told his male analyst that every time the latter talked he was made uncomfortable. The analyst sounded like a politician who was appearing as if he were trying to whip up action and the patient very much resented this. When the patient was asked which politician the therapist reminded him of, the patient with embarrassment mentioned Bella Abzug. "Yes, you are a woman underneath it all. A latent homosexual is what you really are. You should get out of your profession." When the patient was asked what was wrong with being a therapist and a latent homosexual concomitantly, the patient after castigating the therapist for several hours was eventually able to confess that, "I'm not really sure if I'm a man. Sometimes I feel that I have no penis at all! Is that why *I* have to be a loud politician?"

It should be emphasized that the process of analyzing and working with the patient's resistances is not an orderly and smooth process. In practice, therapist and patient move back and forth from layer to layer and from theme to theme, as the patient's presenting resistances shift in response to the changing anxieties engendered by the therapy and by the vicissitudes of the patient's daily life. What is crucial is to meet the patient where he is and to work with resistances so that they will not damage but enhance ego functioning.[6, 11]

In connection with resistances and their analysis, it should also be stressed that analysis of resistances does not remove or destroy them. The use of defenses and resistances is an essential part of normal ego functioning and adaptation. Resolving resistances in psychotherapy tends to remove the pathological need for resistances in relation to the specific unconscious issues being dealt with at a particular point in the course of the therapy.[3]

Zetzel[12] expressed views on the analysis of resistances as follows:

> Successful analysis will not result in the abolition of defenses, but rather in their modification and increased appropriateness. Three changes are of decisive importance: (1) the diminution of instinctual danger will diminish the need for pathogenic defenses; (2) the analysis of ego fixations will have increased the number of available defenses; and (3) the appropriate operation of the modified defenses and the associated release of neutralized instinctual energy will inevitably lead to increased autonomous ego functioning.

## WORKING THROUGH

Anyone who has participated in either a learning or psychotherapeutic experience recognizes that intellectual or emotional modifications in either the mind or the psyche do not take place quickly. Resistance to change is usually quite strong in most people and it takes much time and effort to give up old, habitual ways of resolving problems no matter how maladaptive or self-defeating the means of solution are. Furthermore, new means of handling conflict often feel unsafe and foreign. It was Freud who pointed out that resistances and transference manifestations do not disappear soon after they come on the scene. It is only by persistent analysis of them "that the patient gradually comes to see the true nature of his neurosis and to overcome it."[4]

Resistances emanating from the various parts of the psychic structure constantly assert themselves in subtle and overt forms, in dreams, in acting out, and, of course, in the transference. Not only does the temporary resolution of one resistance lead to the assertion of others, but the same resistance may appear again and again in various forms.

Donald, whom we referred to in our last case example, was not conflict-free after he recognized that he was projecting some of his femininity and castration anxiety on to the therapist. After having painfully recognized some of his passive wishes, he began to fantasize having anal intercourse and fellatio with his male therapist. These wishes were a manifestation of his strong wishes to depend on a strong father. Although he expressed strong conscious resentment towards his father and frequently towards his analyst, this had to be regarded as a resistance against his latent homosexuality.

When the homosexual fantasies and their defense, homosexual fears, were exposed and lived through, the homosexuality could be seen as a regression from and resistance to his oedipal wishes for mother and competition with father. There were many superego and ego resistances erected against his oedipal wishes which had to be resolved. Then, it turned out that Donald had strong resistances towards his oral incorporative wishes to his mother.

Treatment, twice a week individually and once a week in group, took five years. Over time Donald brought out wishes, fantasies, dreams on all levels of development (oral, anal, phallic–oedipal) and resistances of all types (id, ego, superego, transference) to these wishes.

As the patient works through his various resistances there is a slow, gradual growth of awareness of himself as a functioning human being. From his free associations and the relationship with his analyst the patient begins to re-define reality. He sees how his relationships are colored by perceptions and feelings towards his parents, siblings, and significant others. As his distortions are modified through the therapeutic experience, the patient comes to see that his view of reality has been distorted by his emotional preconceptions[2] and poor meeting of his maturational needs.[10] As his resistances become more and more re-solved, he begins to see reality more and more clearly.[2, 3]

## ACTING OUT

Psychoanalytic therapy is a talking therapy. The fundamen-tal rule for the patient to follow is to say everything that comes to mind—thoughts, feelings, memories, fantasies—regardless of how embarrassing or anxiety producing these associations are.[3] During the course of many analyses, the patient, rather than verbalizing his associations acts them out. For example, instead of putting his wishes and fears of engulfment into words, he comes late for an appointment or does not show up at all. Instead of expressing his resent-ment with regard to real or imagined controls placed on him, he may refuse to his pay fee on time, refuse to take the couch, etc. Sometimes, instead of verbalizing sexual feel-ings towards the therapist, the patient may act them out with someone else.

It is the authors' position that acting out *never* facili-tates psychotherapy but interferes with and can retard it. If one of the aims of therapy is for the patient to master his impulses, a situation in which his impulses master him can not be encouraged. That is why we take the position with the patient that acting out is not good for the treatment and suggest to the patient that he try to stop the acting out and tell us what he is thinking or feeling.

Ethel, a 27-year-old patient, came into treatment with a depression, psychosomatic ailments, sexual frigidity, and poor social relationships. Rather early in treatment she formed a very dependent transference relationship with her male therapist and insisted on phoning him in between sessions. When her wish to have phone conversations was not gratified, she absented herself from her therapeutic sessions.

Her therapist told Ethel that when he informed the patient that phone calls were not helpful for treatment, she was obviously very angry at him, but her anger should be put into words, not acted out. For the next several sessions, Ethel told the therapist that he was ungiving, unkind, sadistic, and she hated his "guts." The discharge of her anger lessened her symptoms and she soon became "quite high," so high that she was ready to quit treatment.

The wish to quit treatment was explored and the patient went on to explain that depending on anyone only led to frustrations. She decided, therefore, that she would "do it alone." When the therapist made the interpretation that either Ethel had to resort to excessive demanding or be completely autonomous, she began to bang on the office wall. Again, the therapist advised the patient to put into words what she was feeling and stop banging the wall.

Ethel angrily told the therapist, "I can't win with you. You don't let me be your lovable child and you don't let me leave!" This stirred up memories related to her childhood and she described several incidents in which she either was encouraged to be excessively dependent or excessively independent. The recollection of the memories together with the analyst's stance that acting out was not helpful for the treatment strengthened several ego functions and the treatment moved on quite successfully.

One of the cautions to be noted when the analyst must discourage acting out is that the patient may begin to masochistically enjoy being prohibited. Instead of understanding his wishes for controls, he gets the analyst to offer the controls. If acting out occurs and the analyst discourages it, only to be resumed again by the patient, then an investigation of why the patient likes the therapist's prohibitions must take place. The eventual goal, of course, is that the patient will be able to limit himself when destructive and self-destructive impulses are experienced.

## COUNTERTRANSFERENCE

Just as a successful analysis inevitably necessitates the patient's feeling a variety of affects toward the therapist, such as love, hate, ambivalence, indifference, etc., so too, the therapist has feelings about and toward the patient. As Annie Reich[9] has stated:

> Countertransference is a necessary prerequisite of analysis. If it does not exist, the necessary talent and interest are lacking. But it has to remain shadowy and in the background. This can be compared to the role that attachment to the mother plays in the normal object choice of the adult man. Loving was learned with the mother. Certain traits in the adult object can be seen in its real character and responded to as such. A neurotic person takes the object absolutely for his mother or suffers because she is not his mother.
>
> In the normally functioning analyst we find traces of the original unconscious meaning of analyzing, while the neurotic one still misunderstands analysis under the influence of his unconscious fantasies and reacts accordingly.

Countertransference, then, is part of every analysis. What, of course, has to be differentiated are feelings and affects in the analyst that are induced by the patient, and those reactions of the analyst that are utilized by him to bolster his own defenses. Many young therapists resist experiencing their feelings for fear that this will contaminate the therapy. Nothing could be further from the truth. If the therapist can permit himself to experience his silent feelings and ideas, he can often appreciate what the patient would like to feel but cannot or what the patient would like to receive from the therapist but is afraid to ask for. As the therapist studies his induced feelings, he has to have enough knowledge of his own psyche to recognize what emanates from the patient and what emanates from his own unconscious.

Angry or sexual feelings in the therapist may or may not be in the service of the therapy and have to be constantly scrutinized. Often the therapist can detect in himself inappropriate responses by examining what he does in several hours with the patient. If the analyst returns love with love, hate with hate, over and over again, he is probably failing to detach himself sufficiently from the patient's maturational needs. Such direct responses, when they assume great intensity usually arise from the analyst's unresolved needs.[9]

Occassionally the analyst may get stuck in some of the positions that the patient places him in because they please him too much. Some analysts love to be loved; others love to be hated; others like to deflect feelings toward themselves. When several patients are experiencing the analyst similarly during the same temporal period, the analyst can know that too many of his own needs are pressing in the therapy for expression.

## TERMINATION

When the patient is free "to love and work," when most of his ego functions such as judgment, reality testing, object relations, frustration tolerance, etc., are working well, when he has discarded maladaptive defenses and symptoms, when his thoughts and actions are essentially governed by the reality principle and not by unrealistic fantasies, he is probably ready to terminate treatment.

One of the best clues that the patient is ready to terminate treatment is the transference relationship. When the patient begins to see the therapist more as he is, rather than how the patient would wish him to be, he is probably perceiving other relationships as well as himself realistically. As Freud said, "Where there was id, there is now ego."[4]

It is sometimes overlooked that leaving treatment is psychologically equivalent to death and the patient has the inevitable need to mourn the therapist. Frequently, in order to preserve the treatment relationship the patient regresses to old ways of adaptation, thus convincing himself and the analyst that he should remain in treatment. While the patient should never be rushed out of treatment, it is important to help him confront the fact that staying on in treatment is a residue of the wish to not cut the umbilical cord with mother. Since the patient, after several years of treatment, usually has recognized that clinging dependency is always self-defeating, he is usually able, with the ego strengths acquired, to try his wings in the complex and nonindulgent world.

# Chapter 5

# THE PATIENT IN GROUP TREATMENT

In this chapter we will review our thinking and practice in the treatment of the individual in the group setting. Space does not permit more than a sketchy account of our theory and technique in this modality. The roots of our approach are anchored in the fertile soil cleared by Freud and his followers. As we practice it today, we are heavily influenced also by the work of modern group theoreticians, such as Bion,[2] Ezriel,[3] and Spotnitz.[8]

## THE SCREENING SESSION

In addition to the material on the first interview covered in the previous chapter, in screening for group treatment we focus even more intensely on the interpersonal aspects of the prospective participant's life. During the screening interview we "stay on his level." We do not interpret. Our questions tend to be object-oriented, as distant from his ego as possible in time and space.

Our first question might be "How can a group help you?" We then proceed to clarify verbally, in different words, what he or she is trying to conceptualize.

If the interviewee speaks with ease and freedom, we listen with open attention. We pick out for ourselves the points where the relationship touches on another significant person. We may ask a question about that person or get more information about the incident that is being described. What we are trying to construct in our minds is a picture of how he is related to others in his world, and see how that fits into the way he is relating to us at the moment or will relate to participants in the group in the future.

All too often the interviewee does not know where to start or what to say. He may put it all in a nutshell: "I was born in 1931. Things have had their ups and downs. So I thought I'd try group." Another may say, "I don't know if you can help. I don't know if anyone can help me. In fact, I don't even know why I'm here or if I want help."

These vague presentations alert us to the possibility that we may be dealing with a person who does not know his ego boundaries, who may have reality-testing flaws, and who may decompensate under severe pressure.

Many interviewees are eager to have us actively conduct a structured interview. We may go along with them. We find out the vital statistics: address, phone numbers, highest schooling, siblings, who recommended them, and why the recommendation was made. With many we try to get the earliest visual memories of mother, father, or other caring person.[4] We may also try to find out what feeling the recall of this memory evokes.

> For example, one woman's earliest image of her mother was that of a woman wagging a finger at her, scolding her. The feeling that accompanied this memory was mortification. Using the principles of introjection and extrojection, we expected that as the transference developed, we would find

her behaving like her mother, actively finding fault with peers or ourselves, and also passively replaying the humiliated child in the group setting.

We also seek other unconscious material through daydreams and night dreams. Recurring dreams often give us a picture of basic fears and attempts at mastery by the unconscious ego.

One interviewee reported that he would always be running as hard as he could but would find he was moving in slow motion. He felt himself falling short of his objective, which was to get some place within a reasonable period of time.

This was a brilliant lawyer, a graduate of a prestigious school, who was working in an automotive-parts concern in a position not at all commensurate with his gifts and education. He felt that life was slipping by. To pull himself out of the doldrums, he would make desultory attempts to get a job with a legal firm. These would never quite succeed and he would sink back into the status of an underachiever. Each time he mobilized himself into action he would find his attempts sluggish, inadequate, and clumsy. The more he tried, the more inadequate he felt. His secret view of himself was that he was not up to meeting the professional world on its terms; he was a dud.

In group that is what he presented. All his fears were hidden behind this mechanized facade. Led by the group analyst, the members uncovered his negative view of himself and helped him—through a series of interpersonal experiences—to trust his perceptions and aptitudes, and to chance new ventures without his paralyzing apprehension.

Recurring dreams also have a diagnostic value. They may, for instance, reveal destructive patterns of the interviewee.

A prospective member reported that he had an incessant dream of blowing up the world he was living in, and suffering for it. A little exploration revealed that he was an energetic salesman with much drive who would rack up an enviable record for himself in the first six months on a job, but he would end it by doing something outrageous—often undermining the company for which he was working. This would result in his discharge.

It occurred to us that this might happen to him in the group—he might begin well and then bungle it by engaging in a piece of destructive acting out. He made an immediate positive impression on the members, grasped the emotional language, and was a peer leader within weeks. He worked away at his own and others' difficulties, particularly ferreting out the reasons members acted out or were ducking attention with silence.

At the peak of his popularity, he began to absent himself from sessions. His behavior was at once pointed out to the group. The group analyst actively focused the members' attention on tracing his aberrant behavior back to its starting point. They latched on to his sudden interest in a seductive woman in the group. It was observed that she had been absent from one of the meetings he had missed, but for a seemingly valid reason. One of the insightful members began to probe her new tenseness. She revealed that she had been seeing the salesman outside of group meetings and he had used pressure to keep her quiet. Both were planning to "drop the group thing."

If the analyst had not been alerted by the recurrent dream, buttressed by the subsequent material, the matter would have ended in another fiasco for the patient. But with the group analyst's sustained interest and the concern of his peers, the patient was able to talk about the experience, its attendant feelings, and some of the germane memories that formed this pattern. His membership in the group was preserved. The tendency reappeared a number of times before it was simply felt rather than acted upon.

When we ask for the interviewee's most recent dream, we generally get a dream that occurred the night before. This is not always so. Sometimes it will be a dream culled from the past two or three weeks or months. In any event, we as individuals all look at it carefully. We make the assumption that this dream is telling us about ourselves. It is a message to us, selected by the unconscious processes. We

are portrayed in it and play a part in the dynamics of it.[1]
Though we do not ordinarily ask for associations, through
deductions and reconstructions we can sift out our forthcoming roles in the unfolding interaction with the group
member.

> One interviewee recounted a dream of the previous night.
> She was with a group of cousins whom her father found
> attractive and appealing. She tried to outshine them and get
> his attention by becoming witty and sparkling, but the cous-
> ins became wittier. Frustrated, she changed her attitude and
> became defiant and obstreperous to get his concern. This
> was the drama she later played out in group, substituting
> members for cousins, and the group analyst for her father.

Many candidates for conjoint treatment have been exposed to therapy before. We take a great interest in this
experience, its duration, frequency of visits, and what took
place. We concern ourselves particularly with how the relationship terminated—what took place, what were the dynamics, what did the interviewee think of his therapy and
his therapist? We try to fit the information into what we
have already gleaned from our interview, and attempt to
sense a possible transferential pattern. Foreseeing is fore-
armed. This also helps us select the appropriate group for
the prospective member. If the interviewee has dropped
out because he was overwhelmed by his verbal exhibitionistic peers, it may be one of the factors in our decision to put
him in a relatively subdued group.

> One interviewee had broken off his treatment with a thera-
> pist who was close to his own age. Earlier material had
> indicated to us an intense hostility toward his own siblings.
> The manner in which he had stopped his treatment sug-
> gested that rivalry played a role in it. Other indications—
> particularly his recent dream—showed a need to be close to
> an older figure. He was placed in a group that had both
> peer-age members and mature adults. The two factors bal-

anced each other, and part of the pattern could be worked through in the group initially with the members, and later another part could be dealt with as it emerged again toward the group analyst.

Some of the ground rules for the group experience may be explained to the prospective member, such as the advisability of a six-week trial period to see if the group fits him and if he fits into the group. The option of transferring him to a more efficacious group or treatment modality should this be desirable would be raised at that time. He is told about the fee, and any objections to it are aired and analyzed.

His questions about the forthcoming experience are elicited and answered. If there is any indication of anxiety, this is scrutinized in depth. If it is a matter of reassurance, he is told he does not have to talk in the group sessions until he feels comfortable.

One prospective member agreed to the provisions mentioned by the interviewer, but as she arose to leave she mentioned that it was "all very scary." Though the hour was almost up, the analyst suggested they talk about it. She revealed that she was a self-contained, secretive person. When she spoke in public, she was overwhelmed by anxiety which would show itself in blushing and stuttering. She did not know if she could stand the group exposure. She generally covered her fear by being amenable and compliant, but if she became the cynosure of everyone's interest, the symptoms would return.

The analyst who referred her for group therapy had been aware of her defensive tendency to be a recluse because of this fear. They had worked on it a long time and she had thought she had mastered it. After all, she was now a schoolteacher and a member of a ski-club. But as the group analyst explained how the members communicated to each other, her old apprehensions had crept back with all their original intensity. She had not meant to mention them;

rather, she had formed a plan to call the group analyst later and beg out of meeting the group, using her work schedule as an excuse.

The group analyst suggested that perhaps she was not ready for the experience and would not be ready for it until they found out why she stuttered and what the blushing was trying to say. With the pressure off, she agreed to return for another chat.

The next session was devoted to the sumptoms. What would her vocal chords say if she did not construct consonant hurdles which would interrupt the flow of communication? People sometimes blush when they are exposed or caught doing something not permitted or frowned upon. What could her body be afraid of revealing? What was the arcane message it was trying to send out and hide at the same time?

With some reluctance she associated to these probings. Experiences with masturbation came to her mind. One, in particular, stood out in bold relief. She was playing with her clitoris in the closed closet in her room. Suddenly the door opened and there stood her mother glaring down at her with disapproval. She could not recall what was said to her, but did know it was "hideous."

The analyst suggested that the group would find out something she wanted to keep to herself which was embarrassing.

She poured out a number of masturbatory fantasies which sounded as if they had been served up before and were being warmed over.

He asked what were the rituals that currently gave her self-pleasure.

She immediately blushed and began to stutter. She reached for her handbag and rose.

The analyst told her it was more important for her to put her thoughts and feelings into words, not action. Right now her body was doing the communicating, and body talk was too confusing, primitive, and elusive. It would be better just to sit still until she found her tongue again.

The tension subsided and she began to breathe more easily. She kept her eyes fastened on the purse on her lap. Slowly she began to spell out how she masturbated.

The analyst listened quietly to the anality and "perversity" of it all. When she finished, he wondered aloud what the "big deal was all about."

She stared at him in disbelief. It was difficult for her to accept the fact that someone else would not regard her as a "moral leper."

He wanted to know what was leprous about it. What gave her the idea she was different from the rest of the human race? As far as he could make out, her mind functioned like any other mind. A child does not choose any specific way to get its pleasure. It learns later that there are better ways to get it. There was nothing wrong with her. She was just a product of bad training. All she needed was a little retraining, and even then, she would not have to give up the pleasure she got now unless she wanted to or found something better. And still she could return to it if she ever became dissatisfied.

Her face relaxed. Tears streamed down it unchecked, but it looked ten years younger.

The analyst asked her when she wanted to go into group.

She smiled. "Next week."

To have ignored this anxiety would have been equivalent to losing a potential member, or—if she had forced herself to attend—to courting a potential drop-out.

If the prospective member is seen first by the group analyst, an analyst for individual treatment is recommended. This suggestion is made in terms of the maturational needs of the patient or the impact of a significant figure in his life. The sex of the individual analyst may be important, but more often some other factor revealed by the prospective member determines the choice.

It was clear with one patient that he was traumatized by a cool, distancing relationship with his mother, who was basically frightened of her own feelings. He was referred to a male therapist who had that superficial characteristic. The therapist showed a natural sensitivity to the needs of his patients and could be counted on to respond to their verbal and nonverbal communications with delicacy and tact, and never with neglect, coolness, or "tit-for-tat." Given this opportunity, a working relationship was established between patient and therapist.

Even with all the information gleaned from the screening session it may be difficult to select the right therapist. Two or three names may be given to the interviewee, with the caution that he should trust his intuition and consider the initial contacts as a trial period.

There are times when no recommendation at all is offered. We may find that we cannot make a clear, educated, clinical estimate of the appropriate choice of a conjoint therapist. In this case we wait from four to eight weeks until we have an "experiential feel" of the member, studying his interactions with his peers, how he relates to us, and the topics he talks about in the group setting. The choice made at this point tends to be the right one.

But at no time do we have any compunction about changing the individual or group analyst. We explore a member's complaints or his lack of progress. If the resistance cannot be resolved by insight or by joining, and if it appears to call for interminable working-through, we may recommend or agree to the patient's wish for a different therapist. We are not welded to the premise that all difficulties must be resolved by one set of therapists, one form of treatment, or one school of thought. Our measuring rod is, what will resolve the resistance and facilitate progressive communication? If a recommendation is made that does not work out for the patient, we are interested in the reason only in so far as it will help us make a better one the next time. It is a never ending source of amazement that one patient will do superbly with a particular analyst and another patient with almost similar dynamics will grind to a therapeutic halt with the same analyst.

We have learned over the years that there is little to be

gained by insisting that the patient stay with the group or individual therapist if there is no "fit." Personality complications, adamant objections, and formidable obstacles appear to vanish overnight once we make the change. The same difficulties may rear up again in the patient, but this time he gets a different response or is made acutely cognizant of the fact that this had happened before and could happen again, and what he may have contributed to the stalemate or the dissatisfaction is explicitly clarified for him.

## THE CONTRACTUAL PERIOD

With some sophisticated patients who have had a number of years of individual therapy and others who present a cooperative frame of mind, the contract may be hinted at or explained in the interviewing session. But, generally speaking, the contract is worked out slowly as the interchanges develop in the group.[5] We have general criteria of what is acceptable therapeutic behavior, and we make them known to the patient at the appropriate moments. For example, when a member drifts in ten minutes late, we observe that people in the group are supposed to arrive five minutes before the session begins, not ten minutes after it has started. When a member reaches out and touches a peer, we note that physical contact between members is not helpful to the therapy. We never bring a contractual provision to the group's attention until someone has abrogated or transgressed it.

> When one patient lit a cigarette, the group was informed that there was supposed to be no smoking, eating, drinking, chewing, or any other orally gratifying activity. The member smiled, leaned back on his chair, and sent doughnut-shaped smoke circles up to the ceiling. The analyst said nothing. The other group members prodded him. Wasn't he going to

do something about it? The analyst shrugged. What did they want him to do? The member knew he was breaking a rule. One suggested kicking the member out. Another complained that he was poisoning the air. Others admired and supported the wayward smoker. One girl indicated that she did not mind the smoking as much as the attitude it demonstrated, disdain and contempt. This observation immediately mobilized several peers who supported her view. The smoker denied it. He had to have his cigarette. If he had known there would be no smoking, he would never have joined the group. He would give up his dog before he would give up his cigarettes. His response riveted attention on him. Members began to explore with him what would happen if he gave up his habit for "a whole hour and a half." He tried to muster reasons for holding on to it—he would feel uncomfortable, be silent, develop unnecessary resentment. "Why not ask the members to take off their clothes or sit on the floor? Why pick on smoking?" One member touched on the latent reason, suggesting that the cigarette helped him hide his anxiety and give everyone an impression of self-control; but the group was one place where he could afford to drop his front and be himself. The smoker did not answer. The members picked up on another subject. A few minutes later he stamped out his half-smoked cigarette, drew a deep breath, and began to participate in the new topic under discussion.

Members tend to resent the assumption that they should know the rules that were not spelled out to them beforehand. There is much frustration and acrimonious contention with us on this issue. It is a time when considerable hostility is vented. Though we may experience this as uncomfortable, we are also aware that it helps the group form a cohesive unit. The members have an object for their aggression, feel reasonably justified spewing forth venom, and a sense that they all share a common attitude.

We may bring deviations to their attention, but we rarely forbid any acitivity unless it is dangerous or appears to be leading toward the acting-out of a treatment-destructive pattern.

At the appropriate time, we systematically elucidate our expectations. In general, the contract can be divided into two parts: the guide lines governing communication and the ground rules. There are three provisos which apply to communications:

1. That each member tell his thoughts and feelings toward the other members and why he has them.
2. That each member put into words what he understands about another member.
3. That each member relate the emotionally significant story of his life—past, future, and, particularly, present.

The ground rules embody four conditions:

1. That each member attend all sessions and arrive on time.
2. That each member pay his bills on time.
3. That each member refrain from acting-in[6] or acting-out.
4. That each member preserve the confidence of the other members' identities and the information they reveal.

Each word of each proviso or condition is charged with meaning which has to be elaborated upon as the group interchanges develop and the relationships ravel and unravel.

In point of fact, we expect and accept deviations from the contract. Once the members know what is expected of them, we watch their reaction to the information. Some are compliant and punctilious about obeying every term of the contract. Others are defiant, forgetful, contentious, undecided, or sporadically cooperative. Each response is studied for its significance and silently analyzed. We ask ourselves: Why is this or that behavior taking place at this time? What does it mean?

Our verbal activity is devoted to focusing on the group resistance,[7] that is, the attitude or behavior that the members share which abrogates the "agreement." A few may express the reluctance openly, with the covert complicity of a silent majority.

Upon entering the meeting room, the group analyst found a check on his seat. He picked it up and observed aloud that payment was supposed to be made at the end of the last session of the month, not at the beginning of the next month. The member who had placed the check there mumbled a lame excuse about forgetting to bring his checkbook to the meeting before. The other group members ignored the issue.

The following payment time was treated the same way, only this time there were four checks on his chair.

The analyst repeated his original statement. One teacher quipped that she got paid every fortnight on a Friday the day after the group meeting. It was the fault of the Board of Education, which had not yet adjusted itself to the analyst's rules. The members chuckled. No one offered any other rationale for the late payments.

The following month, one member did not pay at all, and had to be reminded. Another gave only a partial payment. Two members sent in their checks by mail.

Each time the analyst brought the matter to the group's attention, it seemed to exacerbate the lackadaisical tendency. The five regular-paying members seemed indifferent to this aberration and to the analyst's concern with it. One of them noted that there were priorities in one's life, and paying for analysis came after such things as rent, food, medical bills, and carfare.

The analyst observed that perhaps they could not afford group therapy. After all, clinics were available, and the groups that met there cost only half the price of his sessions. Two members immediately recounted their "weird" experiences in a clinic group. They did not want to deal with "amateurs" again. One of the tardy payers acknowledged he would see to it that his check was there on time. The rest were silent.

The inevitable confrontation occurred when a member

arrived back from a two-week vacation and announced he would not be able to pay for the two sessions he had missed.

The analyst said he would be charged for them. No one could be put in his place while he was absent. It was like buying a box at the opera—he paid for the chair even if he was not there.

The member admitted he knew all of this before he left, but had decided he needed the money for the plane fare. He would compromise: he would catch up on his payments during the summer, while the analyst was on vacation. But for the present, he was short of funds and would have to withhold the check for that month.

The analyst asked the group what the members thought about the fact that he was now considered the convenient banker for vacations and other services. No one responded.

The analyst noted that no one seemed interested in the problem except himself. Since he was an analyst and not a moneylender, perhaps the members did not need him. It might be that the group should be disbanded.

This thought mobilized the five steady payers. They saw no reason why they should suffer because half the members were "dawdling deadbeats."

The analyst wanted to know why not. Were they a group or were they not? If they were a working group, they would see to it concertedly that they conducted themselves as a group. One thing was certain: as a group, they did not seem to consider it important when or if he got paid.

The five concerned members wanted to know what they could do about someone else's haphazard payments. They had no control over "checkbook creeps." The analyst suggested that they could at least try to find out why they themselves were uninterested in the phenomenon. What did they get out of ignoring this deviation?

What they then revealed was a private pleasure in seeing the authority figure defied, and the rules twisted and flouted. They had understood what the late payers were doing when they put the checks on his chair. It was an expression of contempt for the analyst. It was like saying "Up yours!" They had been waiting to see how he would handle each challenge.

When they understood their passive participation, they turned on the defaulters. True enough, the latter were testing to see how far they could go. What was the analyst's boiling point? When would he "lose his cool?"

Once the defaulters felt free to talk about their testing and defiance, they let loose a blast at the analyst. He was called rigid, inflexible, and "plagued with a picayune preoccupation" with details, all designed to restrict their freedom.

Various views emerged as each member dealt with the group theme. Lurking behind all the activity and the complaints were both the wish for the leader to set limits, and the fear of his imagined power, a fear that was concretized when he mentioned that he might break up the group.

Group resistances are dealt with first. Then we deal with subgroup resistances and, finally, with individual difficulties, as they reflect the group tendency to hinder or distort interpersonal communication. If need be, we engage in one-to-one exchanges in an emergency.

The major group resistances are discussed in the next chapter.

# Chapter 6

# MAJOR GROUP RESISTANCES

In this chapter we will discuss five major group resistances: treatment-destructive, status quo, progress, teamwork, and terminal.

## TREATMENT-DESTRUCTIVE RESISTANCES

We have other priorities as well. These deal with what we might call the sequential resistances. The most serious of these are the treatment-destructive resistances. Many patients enter groups destined to be drop-outs. Before relationships develop, when they are on the verge of developing, or even because they are developing, they act in a manner calculated to break up the therapy. This may be a reenactment of other disastrous disruptions in their lives; it may have its basis in a fathomless fear of imminent intimacy; it may be their usual way of relating to the world, be it job, spouse, school, or objectives. This was seen in the example of the salesman who during this initial interview revealed in a recurring dream his tendency to self-destruct.

Nor does the phenomenon stop there. Any activity that threatens the integrity of the group; undermines its continuous existence; jeopardizes the membership, the physical being, or health of any member; or negatively influences the setting in which the members work so that they can no longer function effectively in it comes under the category of a treatment-disruptive resistance. It can emanate from ego, superego, id, secondary gain, or transference. It can be charged with aggressive or libidinal energy coming from any stage of development: oral, anal, urethral, oedipal. Each of these factors has to be taken into consideration because from whence it comes determines what the group analyst does in each case.

The attitude and the countertransference of the leader also play a critical role in this resistance pattern.[1] Many a member has been allowed to act out his tendency in this direction because the analyst either ignored it or made only half-hearted attempts to deal with it. In his mind, the analyst may have decided that this was not a patient he liked, admired, or wanted to have in his practice; or he may have developed a rage at the patient's provocativeness which he denied to himself, trying to circumvent his own unacceptable feeling, instead of using it to confront the patient. Because he does not recognize his own feeling, he cannot make constructive use of the conjoint colleague relationship. What sometimes transpires is that the individual conjoint analyst is not even alerted to the oncoming rupture from the group or, at best, hears about it vaguely through the patient's idiosyncratic version of what is going on.

What are the telltale signs of an incipient imperilment to the group experience? A usually punctual member suddenly begins to arrive late; a member overlooks telephoning that he cannot attend the meeting, what is more, he does not mention his absence at the next session; a member

falls behind in his payments, but offers no plausible explanation; a member starts to find fault with the group room
—its chairs, pictures, atmosphere, or location; a member
begins to "forget" the day of the meeting, the time, even
the place; a member complains that the group confuses
him, upsets him, or makes him lose his grip on reality.

This list can be extended indefinitely. We have mentioned only some of the more visible resistances. The dead-
lier ones are the silent, insidious ones that build up. We are
not aware of them until it is too late: when the member
announces at the end of a group session that he is not
coming back, or when he disappears without a word. Some
of these patients just leave a message with the analyst's
answering service, while the meeting is in progress, to the
effect that they are not returning, or they have someone
else call for them with this news. A few have sent letters or
notes while on vacation.

The perplexing fact may be that the member has appeared to be sincere, committed, and cooperative. We may
have no idea that he has reached the conclusion that his
peers are too educated, too advanced, too fast, too lower
class, or too slow. Occasionally we are fortunate enough to
hear of these eliminating evaluations from the conjoint
analyst or from other members to whom the phrase is
dropped as they are leaving the room or waiting for a bus.

But if we keep ourselves in a state of therapeutic alert-
ness, there are subtle suggestions of a potential withdrawal
from the group. For example, instead of touching on the
seven vital subjects—present life, past events, future plans,
dreams, sexual life, feelings toward peers, and ideas about
the group leader—the member deals with only one issue or
evades them all with a noncommittal attitude toward others. Any member who has not broached any of these subjects during the six-week trial period may be questioned as
to why he has not mentioned a particular subject. When a
member does not seem to be taking one part, that is, his

expected share, of the total talking time after the second session, the matter is brought to the group's attention. Any member who does not engage in meaningful interchanges is studied carefully for unspoken reservations that make for interpersonal distancing. Silence is always suspect, particularly if we sense that it is accompanied by discomfort or anxiety. We accept as axiomatic that there is no hiding place in the shared-treatment setting.

The treatment-destructive resistance can take a thousand mutant shapes, but we find that the most important points to keep in mind about this pattern are:

1.   The attitude never gets a chance to be aired and explored.

2.   The member tends not to have a definite object on which he might vent his dissatisfaction.

3.   The feeling behind the breach is often shrouded in vagueness and denial.

What is of critical import is that once the resistance is sensed, it must be heeded. Not to respond to it may mean that the member is on his way out the door, as far as treatment is concerned. In fact, everything else that is occurring in the group takes a back seat. This becomes the first order of business. There is never any therapeutic justification for postponing the confrontation of a treatment-destructive resistance. Whatever measures the leader takes at this point must be considered necessary and urgent. The objective is to preserve the group relationship for the member.

First of all, the analyst may call the group's attention to the resistance. He may point out that the behavior can reflect a group problem, or that the group may be failing the member by not meeting his needs. [2] The group leader may wonder aloud if he has not succeeded in making some point of the contract clear and may spell it out again. He may focus the members' interest on the behavior itself.

Perhaps it is trying to say something? What could it be? Does any member have any idea?

Most of all, the member himself is helped to talk about the aberrant behavior. Its history may be explored. If the member is on an oedipal level of development, it may be interpreted. If it emerges from the oral or anal stage of development, it may be joined or reflected. If the member's ego can not tolerate self-examination, the focus is kept away from it.

> One member with a wobbly sense of self started to slip into the session 25 minutes after it started. She claimed that her bus arrived late. She was always at the terminal on time. No progress was made with her lateness until the analyst agreed with her. She had nothing to do with the delay. It was a "bus resistance." At the next session she was on time. The tendency came back occasionally, but would always correct itself if it was discussed as a "bus resistance." No effort was made to get around or repress the resistance. There was no attempt at any ego confrontation. She was merely helped not to act on her general treatment-destructive pattern. The second sign was that she was dropping out of courses which she had started at her local community college. She had decided it was a chore to get there and she was arriving late for classes. The group picked up the analyst's interest in her decision. After a while, each time the members saw emergent signs of such acting-out, they were able to circumvent any urge toward tardiness on her part. The pattern was not approached analytically until her ego boundaries had firmed and it had become a full-blown transference resistance. Then it responded to other interventions and working-through.

## THE STATUS QUO RESISTANCE

Once the treatment-destructive resistances are temporarily resolved and most of the conditions of the contract have been accepted, a group appears to trot along at a brisk pace for about six to eight months. Members work on each other's difficulties, and they establish viable relationships with each other. Then the therapeutic trot slows down to an amble, and soon it seems that the group is meandering aimlessly like a leaderless pack of horses, browsing here and there but going nowhere in particular.

Yet the members enjoy being together. They look forward to each meeting. They have all adjusted their lives to attend the "Wednesday session." It is as much a part of their thinking as going to school or brushing their teeth. Without giving it a second thought, they have rearranged their work and recreation to get there at the right time. They express appreciation of the analyst's communications. They admire the work that went into the design of the meeting room. They like the idea that they have this interpersonal island where they can drop the cliches and social veneer of everyday life. They begin to look on themselves as an unusual gathering of people, who are fortunate to have found each other.

It appears that a salutary cohesive process has taken place. In fact, all looks well, and most short-term group therapy stops here. But a closer look reveals that angry, envious, or negative feelings have been relegated to the unspoken limbo of the "unacceptable." There is a covert concurrence not to uncover anything that threatens the present détente.

When a member brings up some on-going personal problem, his part in the drama he regales them with is not pointed out to him. Instead, he may be given some practical advice. He is even more apt to receive ample emotional support, compassion, and psychological alignment. The other members are on his side to a man.

What has happened appears to be a paradox. They have stopped moving forward, but they are not unpleased about it. The elusive truth is that the members are satisfied with what has taken place within themselves and their lives to-date. They want to keep the even tenor they have attained, hold things as they are. They do not want change. If they upset the established balance in the group setting, there is no telling what will be upset inside themselves and their real life. Thus, there is a marked need to let things go along as they are, coupled with a reluctance to act in any new direction. The members seem committed to coasting contentedly, squeezing out secondary gains from their therapeutic quiescence.

Group pressure appears to be exerted in the direction of conformity. Members squelch anyone who might go against the prevailing trend. Any impatient push ahead is curbed. Emergence of meaningful new material or feeling is suppressed. On the positive side, effort will be made to get a member to arrive on time by ganging up on him. The obstreperous member who interrupts everyone may be whipped into line. The shouter may be toned down until he speaks in a civilized manner.

But in terms of group progress, nothing is happening. What is more, nothing appears to budge the members. The novitiate group therapist begins to question his ability to conduct such a group; or he overcompensates by enthusiastically whipping up activity with provocative interventions. Failing that, he finally settles down to doing individual therapy in the shared setting. He selects one member in need or responds to someone's craving for attention and concentrates his counseling concern on him. If he is fortunate, some members of the group join in to aid him, as long as it does not upset the overall equipoised equanimity.

If the superficial banter is allowed to continue, it can turn into a treatment-destructive pattern. Since no one is making progress in the group setting, some members begin to feel an urge to move outside it. They may announce new plans. A few may find that they have garnered as much as they can get out of the treatment.

Whenever we detect a doldrum, we look for corrobora-

ting external evidence. What is going on? What is not happening? Detection is the most important step. The next
step is investigation. What is the cause of this inertia? The
third step calls for devising a procedure to resolve the
stalemate. Depending on the development of the group or
a member of the group, we can join the status quo resistance; that is, we may go along with it verbally, or we can
confront and interpret it, using what leverage the transference affords us at the moment.

Ten blacks, comprising six "nationalists," two pimps, and
two prostitutes, were sent by the courts to group therapy
with the warning that if they unilaterally terminated treatment, they would immediately lose their parole status.

This warning discouraged any treatment-destructive
acting-out, but did nothing to ameliorate a protracted hostile phase that was accompanied by great difficulties in establishing a working agreement. The therapist's interventions,
designed to set up the analytic contract, were rejected out
of hand. They served as excuses for mob-like upheavals. If
he persisted, he was assaulted with racist clichés and four-
letter invectives. Reasoning with these patients was as ex-
hausting as it was fruitless.

It was only when he joined their rebellious attitude,
using the ideas they presented, that they began to formulate
some rules of behavior. For example, one member did not
show up for a meeting. This upset the others because the
judge's warning still rang in their ears. At the next session,
when they wanted to know what had happened, the wan-
derer was evasive. The analyst leaped to his defense with all
kinds of rationalizations for his absence. This mobilized the
group's negative attitude toward the therapist. They made
it a rule that everyone must "report in." They took full credit
for the innovation, translating the analyst's suggestion into
their own slang.

When they were convinced that the analyst accepted the
position that he was an outsider and knew nothing, they felt
willing to give him a "picture of what they were all about."
They took on a superior teacher role in relation to him. This
did not prevent brushfires of fury from flaring up each time

they associated him with the establishment. Their fear, contempt, and hatred of the "white think-shrink" mellowed somewhat as he persistently met their abuse with silence or, when it was called for, an honest, forthright response.

One can imagine the relief the therapist experienced when the members entered a productive period of personal interchanges which converted them from a callous, vengeance-venting gang into a charismatic "combo" of sparkling personalities. Their insights into each other's intentions and motivations were nothing less than awesome. They never allowed themselves to be hoodwinked by any one member or subgroup. No one could hide from their dry wit. Behind their sharp probes was an intense positive interest in each other. Everyone felt this concern.

The group meeting would begin about two minutes before the therapist entered the room. In colorful, colloquial language, a member would "roll out" a rollicking account of how he had dealt with, or outwitted, society, employer, friend, or foe that week. These were hilarious episodes.

Buried in the details of the tale there was always some personal issue that had not been met. Members easily picked it up and, amid acrimonious arguments, gave admirable advice on the best course of action and where the member had failed to take it. They goaded balking members who did not feel they had the courage, ability, or aptitude to take the needed steps to get where they wanted to go.

For example, in order for the prostitutes to move out of the "trade," they had to make new contacts and friends. This put them at loggerheads with their pimps, who tried to take occupational possession of them by any means, adroit or foul. The procurers in the group anticipated every move along with the strategy to counter it. The nationalists fueled the prostitutes fight for freedom with appeals to their black dignity, and provided them with an unusual understanding of the needs that precipitated them into this "slavery." All but two members made substantial changes under this concerned plotting and prodding. Several members, surprised at their newfound strength, began to sense the possibility of something more in the world for them. A few entered conjoint treatment to get further into "sticky stuff."

The status quo resistance began to appear in force as the meetings took on a homey character. Members, addressing each other as "brothers" and "sisters," were warm and friendly. They found the sessions "cool coming to" and talked about how much they "dug" being together. Though it never burst into acting-out, a lot of good-natured erotic teasing kept the proceedings bubbling along. There was a frequently discussed plan for a party when the "shrink" took his vacation. They found themselves attached to the group room which they had initially labeled "the parole prison." Coming to the sessions indefinitely would offer them no problem.

As they smoothed out their interpersonal clashes, so did they minimize any sign of inner psychological conflict within themselves. The fascinating jousts with external reality took a mundane turn, centering on job changing, "laying out" landlords, and other relatively superficial matters.

No urgent difficulties developed. If prodded, their response was that "things were going great on the street." Dreams and fantasies which might offer access into their turbulent psyches were conspicuously absent.

Their aggression seemed to have vanished. Even the talk of it was hollow and half-hearted. The nationalists still held that the streets would "run red," but one got the idea that there had been a postponement. The intensity of their feelings on the subject had turned to a pale pink. They explained this by saying they were "moving the mountain instead of blowing it up." They easily managed to land jobs with activist social agencies which used their uncommon skills, while enabling them to release some of their protest energy.

All in all, the members were content with the distance they had come, and were more than willing to ride on a self-satisfied tide. What efforts they exerted were in the direction of keeping the level of their interchanges on an even keel. Gone was the lively explosive response to the therapist. In its place was muted admiration for his ability to "take it and be cool."

Thus they sailed along for two months. The therapist, scarred by the stinging early sessions, was in a counterresistant state of bliss. He marveled at their growth and found in each of them something to be admired and enjoyed. He did not realize that the sessions had taken on a repetitive pattern, lacking any progressive communication in depth.

The awkward awakening took place when a member

announced that the group had certainly helped him, and because of this, he had decided to take a course in political science at Hunter College which he had been delaying for years, the only hitch was that it conflicted with the group's meeting time. Would the analyst speak to his parole officer about substituting the course for therapy for the coming semester? This unilateral decision suggested that something was amiss. The following week two other members came in with similar ingenious schemes.

Between sessions the analyst went over the group's development, and it became clear to him that he had permitted their euphoric honeymoon. They had sidestepped frightening inner areas they did not want to get into, and he had avoided treading on the dragon's tail of their aggression, luxuriating in acceptance by the members. Consultation with some of their individual analysts confirmed his conclusions.

At the following session, another member proposed a project that would prevent her from attending the meetings. The analyst said he thought all the plans were good ones and he would speak to the parole people. Only one thing bothered him: none of them had expressed any interest in what he thought about their idling along.

At once they were up in arms. They took umbrage at the word "idling." They had been "working, man, working!" Things had never been better in their lives. "Where did he get off with that shit?" they asked each other. They were doing exactly what he wanted them to do—"making it!"

The analyst agreed they might be right. But where did the analyst get the idea that they wanted him to turn their therapy group into a social club in which members could drift in and out at their convenience without consulting him beforehand?

The storm intensified. They protested that there was nothing superficial about their group. Where was his head anyway; whose idea was it that they should get jobs, better themselves? they asked. They had come hating the group "shit" and had grown to like the experience. "What the hell else do you want?" they wanted to know.

The analyst said nothing while they spewed forth their spleen. When they had finished, he summarized what they had said and thanked them for attributing their improvement to him. But were the changes enough? It appeared to him that there was a lot of self-deception going on, which allowed them to avoid undertaking an upsetting search within themselves. They contemplated this thought. Why should they take the scabs off old sores? The past was dead and buried, as it should be. The analyst explained that he was not interested in history either. It seemed to him, however, that they had a richer potential than they presented. But to find it, they would have to go forward into unknown terrain and examine the uncertainties they were sweeping under their psychological carpets. Every time it looked like someone was going to pick up the rug, he was sat on instead of helped. No one seemed interested in what such a member was trying to say. To take one example: when W. started to talk about tracking down his real father, and finding out what had happened to him, everyone told him to forget it. No one wanted to consider what was pushing Whisper to turn detective. And, again, no one remarked on the way M. turned down J. when he began to edge toward her and talk about his real feelings.

After some five illustrations, the protesting petered out. The members regarded each other uncertainly.

In the next meeting no one mentioned any new plans. There was some search into the hidden motives for the group's status quo resistance. Fantasies began to emerge about "being in an easy place." The members' lives had been a disruptive stream of episodes. They had found an island of peace and equilibrium in the group. They wanted to hold on to it. To venture further was fraught with fear. They were now poised hesitantly on the threshold of entering sensitive areas between themselves and within themselves.

## RESISTANCES AGAINST PROGRESS

With the black group, a new phenomenon appeared. The verbal gamboling vanished; an air of tentativeness replaced the original ebullience; and long, furtive silences marked each meeting. It seemed that this highly intelligent collection of personalities was uncertain of its direction and unable to get bearings or chart a course of communication. When the group analyst brought this new twist to their attention, members wanted to know what they could do about it. Their newfound ignorance was a way of avoiding a venture into the unknown. They could not be accused of refusing to move ahead if they did not know what course to take. Asking for a way to do something was equivalent to seeking a safe way, one that would not lead to unforeseen consequences.

If members insisted on guidance and the analyst told them what to do, they would have difficulty putting the information to therapeutic use. They either misconstrued what was said or rendered the instruction innocuous by staying on the surface. If asked, "What do you feel toward W.?" the answer might only be "He's solid, knows the score." When nothing much happened, the analyst was apt to be accused of giving them the wrong directions.

This is universally true of groups bogged down in a resistance against progress. There is much anxiety in this phase, quantitatively four to five times more than in the status quo state.

There is a great fear of change underlying this lack of direction. Members are afraid to take the steps that will move them toward the unfamiliar state of real mental equanimity. They have never associated with a stable world. They do not know what to expect, yet they are not content with the tranquility they have just left behind. Therefore, impediments appear at every turn. No one wants to say what has to be said to another member regardless of consequences. They say, in essence, "You tell me what to say. You take the responsibility for it."

Many therapists resort to dealing with each member's anxiety singly. They ignore the shared experience. It becomes a matter of giving individual treatment in the group setting as a member's anxiety attracts attention.

Other therapists persist in acceding to the group's calls for counsel and guidance.

We find it more fruitful to counter the demands for direction by indicating that it is more important to study how the members are evading emotional issues between one another and ourselves. The seesaw struggle between sticking to safe subjects and the attraction to new ones is used as an opportunity to uncover and resolve gripping personality patterns. Let us look in some detail at a group in a state of resistance against progress.

A therapist discontinued his practice in the city, attaching himself to a hospital some 90 miles away. He gave his one group, which was in combined treatment with him, a list of possible leaders, and after interviews they made their selection. Most of them entered into conjoint treatment, for the group analyst saw no one individually.

They were a tightly knit community that had worked together for years. When first seen by their new analyst, they assembled weekly, more from the force of habit and personal attachment than from any drive to deal with their interpersonal difficulties. They saw the individual session as the primary arena for working out intimate difficulties.

The intermember webs they had woven in the group occasionally wavered with a gust of strong feeling, but kept the basic symmetrical shape. There was an inner subgroup that was strongly linked together, an outer subgroup that switched allegiance between one or two members, and two peripheral figures whom all others ignored most of the time, but supported when they presented problems with their families and spouses.

Though there had been little progress within the last year or so, they were in consensual agreement that the group had been a valuable experience for which they were grateful. In all essentials, they presented a group status quo resistance.

After waiting until they had accustomed themselves to him, the new analyst tried to address their shared reluctance. He asked them how they thought he felt about their endless discussion week after week of the same people with the same problems. Did they imagine he wanted them to do this? If so, what could he gain from letting them drift along? The interlocking network of responses that supported this pattern fell apart under his persistent probing.

But instead of moving toward progressive communications, the members experienced this "prying" as reviving old ghosts they thought they had laid to rest. They felt themselves sinking back into their old misery. They had come for, and had gotten, relief from their symptoms, and the new group leader was sanguinely offering them suffering again.

At first there was much talk of "checking out" other group therapists. There were even two exploratory interviews with other professionals. When the group analyst suggested that they were not running away from him so much as fleeing feelings they did not like in themselves, this plan of action was dropped.

The members now regressed to talking about outside events and real-life problems. The group analyst did not nibble at this bait. Their urgent calls for assistance went unheeded. The analyst merely referred such problems back to the other members. He knew that if he helped them deal with these external issues, he would be abetting their avoidance of the anxiety attendant to treading on new psychological terrain, and postponing the day when the transference resistance to him, as the one who was exacerbating their anxieties, would have to be confronted.

The members suggested that he was less than helpful to them. Unfavorable comparisons were made with their first group therapist, who had "always pitched in" to deal with their dilemmas. The group analyst merely wondered aloud why he was so ungiving.

After much speculation about his stinginess, the members decided they had not given him the right kind of information. After all, he did not know much about them. A mass of information was volunteered that was mostly autobiographical in nature. The responses of the other members confirmed the analyst's suspicion that there was nothing really new here. When it was new—coming from the members' present-day experinece—it was presented for its "shock effect." There was a heavy stress on sex and sexual experiences. Even when this pattern was explained to them, it was never integrated in a way that that would indicate true insight.

It was evident that this outpouring was an unconscious maneuver to circumvent the unpredictable. The leader kept making each of these diversionary tactics apparent to the members as they arose.

The ambivalence became more manifest. They wanted to push forward and at the same time did not want to do so. Their misery propelled them forward, and their fear fostered reservations. Concomitantly, there were severe bouts of indecision about moving on to new jobs, dropping old boy friends, taking summer vacations in Europe, or signing up for Ph.D. orals. This displacement was explained to the group as a way of avoiding more critical material in the here-and-now.

A spate of somatizing broke out: protracted colds, unabating low-level fever, inexplicable upset stomachs, and headaches. These were offered as excuses for not attending sessions or for taking a less than active role in the interchanges. Though this phenomenon was described as the body expressing the feelings the psyche was denying, the acting-out persisted. Only when the analyst examined each symptom separately—asking for example, what the headache was trying to say—did these excuses dissipate. They were supplanted by bizarre acting-in, such as, members addressing each other and forgetting the other's name. To those who wondered about it, it was described as a way of forgetting something they might say to each other. They did not want to unmask their uneasy attitudes.

The analyst asked what their objections were to saying anything, no matter what ensued. There were many rationalizations, and much apprehension. The more disturbed members resorted to more primitive defenses as their anxiety increased. One of them had to be helped out of a disassociated state by the others. He began a strange neological string of associations during one meeting. The rest of the members demanded that he make sense. This infuriated him, but after venting his rage, he became more rational.

Many declared they had said all there was to say to each other. Their indecision seemed to go on interminably. Members sarcastically observed that what the analyst told them about themselves did not help much in group, but did help them in their daily existence. Other members found that they were helpful to others in their lives, but had not been helped themselves. In fact, it seemed to them that the analyst was in no hurry to help them.

The group analyst took this cue and queried why they thought he did not want to help them. They evaded the question. He moderated his approach and asked how they would like to be helped. Some said they would like to be left alone; others, that there were too many insights; and still others wished he would stop pointing out their evasions and what they were trying to avoid.

The analyst agreed with them. He admitted that perhaps it was not necessary to say everything they felt about each other or the analyst. There was no pressure to make progress. They had a right to take all the time they wanted. He would sit with them as long as they wished.

This joining procedure elicited a lot of defiance from some who were negatively suggestible. For some it was an invitation to produce information that was used for ulterior purposes, such as manipulating, seducing, teasing half-revealingly, to get attention. None of it developed into constructive communication. For others, it made the situation less threatening. But, in all, it was the final straw that broke the back of the group resistance. The majority felt they had been in treatment long enough. They were tired of the game being played by the analyst. They criticized him for keeping them in a state of uncertainty. What did he really want? He replied, "The truth. The ungarnished details about me, and about each other." They proceeded to give him a picture of himself that was a mixture of fantasy and fact.

When other members sifted out their feelings toward the analyst they turned their attention to each other. Hoped-for exchanges took place between them. Hidden agendas surfaced, and unfinished business let itself be seen. Most of the communications were new in both content and quality. Overblown fears about being worthless, disliked, and unacceptable were punctured. As the analyst interpreted the group and subgroup hesitancies, a strong positive transference toward him emerged. The anxiety level dropped. The group as a whole moved into the rapids of uncharted waters.

When starting a new group, we are always tempted to deal with the progress resistances first, postponing work on

the treatment-destructive designs or the status quo quag-
mires. The anxieties and immediacies of the members cry
out for our reassurance. But it has been our experience that
giving primacy to the resistances to progress at the expense
of the contract, interpersonal cohesion, the group phenomenon, and awareness of the inevitable doldrums, leads to a
turbulent start-and-go experience punctuated by premature terminations. Playing group therapist by ear does not
lead to an orderly group.

We have found still another reason to avoid an initial
emphasis on the progress resistances. Group treatment can
work quickly. Members may manifest improvements in a
relatively short period. The more impressed they are with
the rewards of the treatment, the less apt they are to talk
about their negative feelings toward their group peers or
the leader. As the aggression builds up inside them, they
fear the consequences of letting it out.

One way they may choose to resolve such a dilemma
is to get rid of the burden by terminating treatment on
some logical pretext. If they tend to be self-destructive,
they may fragment their functioning or act precipitously to
eliminate themselves from the group.

This tendency to bottle up hostility is activated particularly in members who in any event tend to sit on aggressive impulses when they are "pushed." With such patients
it is more efficacious to deal first and foremost with the
tendencies to move toward the dissolution of relationships
and not concern ourselves with their push to progress.

## TEAMWORK RESISTANCES

When a group approaches its working maturity, a particular
phenomenon is apparent to an alert observer. Here and
there is a member who regards himself as individually distinct and separate from the rest. His view is that the group
exists for his own benefit. He has little concern for it and

assumes no responsibility for the integrity of its functioning. Such a member will tend to address most of his comments to the therapist. He assumes that the expert will
ultimately resolve his difficulties, so why bother with peers?
They may help in a febrile fashion, but the true omnipo-
tence lies with the analytic shaman.

This insular attitude is often supported by the knowledge that he can ask for a private session to probe into the
matter of personal meaning with the group analyst. Thus,
resistances to teamwork are more apt to arise and persist
when the same therapist is seeing the patient in both individual and group treatments.

There are many sources for this resistance to working
with others. As mentioned, there may be the expectation
that the doctor has the cure-all up his sleeve and, with a
prestidigitator's deftness, will somehow produce the insight at the perfect moment that will free the member from
his neurotic bondage. The resistance may reside in an abid-
ing sibling rivalry that has been fostered by others in the
past so that the member is merely continuing this condi-
tioning in the present setting. It may be due to an identification with an indifferent figure: someone did not care for
him, was not concerned enough to set limits or show him
the appropriate way to work and play harmoniously with
other children. Thus, he is only doing unto others what was
done unto him.

A frequent cause of this cooperation block is the transferential disappointment with the therapist himself. He
does not help the member the way he expected to be
helped. Therefore, why should he cooperate with the expert? Sometimes it is vocalized to the group therapist:
"Why should I do what you want me to do? Why should
I knock myself out figuring out others? I came here, paid
you good money, and you expect me to do your work?
Nuts!"

More often this reluctance is displaced onto his peers.

It can be silently rationalized as "I do not want to help these characters. I despise them. The less I have to do with them, the better." Behind this arrogant attitude may be the fear that he is not able to understand and approach the other members if he tried. An attempt would only make him look the fool.

He may justify his reluctance on the grounds that his peers "are just lazy, acting dumb, playing the old manipulating, 'I'm weak, I can't do it' game. A lie. They can do it, but they want someone else to do the work. The hell with them. If they don't want to do the job, they don't get crocodile tears from me. They can swill in their confusion by their lonesomes. If worse comes to worst, the analyst will have to earn his bread—bail them out." And so the excuses for noncooperation proliferate and pyramid, taking the mutable shapes that fit any given situation.

Occasionally a teamwork resistance affects an entire group. Then it stands out in conspicuous relief. Few or none of the members demonstrate any esprit de corps. Whatever partial identifications they have made with each other or the leader have not resulted in group unity. What concerns one member does not necessarily concern the others. The members find they are not "on the same wavelength" and, what is more, they may not care: If a member does not show up for the meeting, that is his or her business; if a member never involves himself in the on-going theme of the moment, "Too bad"; should a new member be introduced, he may be left to find his own way.

The analyst gets the impression of a competitive society in which laissez faire is the rule rather than the exception. Each member cultivates his own psychological plot of ground and lets the other members take care of their particular needs. Barring a common inconvenience or threat which might cause them to close ranks, each will tend to go his own way or the way of a subgroup with which he aligns himself.

After a series of presentations in a clinical setting, a number of professionals who were in the audience decided collectively to come to the lecturer for training. They wanted to learn the principles of group treatment, both experientially and technically. Though they all stated that it was for the purpose of broadening their therapeutic horizons and increasing their skills, they quickly revealed they had many problems with patients, difficulties with colleagues and the clinic director, and were particularly concerned with the countertransference nets in which they got enmeshed with the groups they conducted.

In the beginning they were favorably predisposed toward the group analyst, attentive and alert to what he was doing. They displayed a lively curiosity about the reason behind each of his interventions. Soon they were working on each other's professional functioning. With singular perspicacity they cleared away much of the countertransference underbrush impeding each member.

The director of the clinic met the analyst at a party and, with a newfound respect for "the group phenomenon," related the change in the working climate of the clinic. In-group battling between the various schools of treatment the therapists advocated had evaporated; the usual complaints, back-stabbing, and time-schedule skirmishes had decreased in intensity and quantity; turnover in patient load had diminished; and new programs were being initiated with minimal "mumbo-jumbo and delaying tactics."

The upheavals in the work setting may have subsided, but the analyst had a totally different experience in the group. What they had stopped doing outside the sessions, the members were doing inside them in a more idiosyncratic way.

A member would ask a question and another would break in before he could get an answer or could take the communication further.

Intense confrontations, frequently with cutting criticisms, would take place between members close to the end of a session. Before the feelings could be resolved satisfactorily, the meeting time would be over. The next session, one or both of the disputants would not appear or would arrive so late that a new on-going theme would prevent picking up the suspended thread. If the thread was singled out again, an animated argument would break out as to what had priority—the here-and-now or the "overhang." A subgroup always remained dissatisfied with the outcome.

Any feasible excuse was used to break up the flow of the sessions. In the midst of another's presentation, a member was apt to recall a pressing problem he had vowed to himself to present at that session. Pauses were unknown because there seemed to be a line-up waiting to be heard. It was not the interchange of the moment that mattered, but the one that was to follow. With all the discursive jumping around, there was no resolution of anything, be it a problem or a give-and-take. The sessions just rushed along helter skelter at a reckless pace with much struggle and little accomplishment.

Under the guise of being a "helpful helper," there was a lot of exhibitionistic activity. Many of the members were all too willing to "expertize" in order to display their skill and put the recipient down in a not-so-subtle fashion. This only added to the intolerable interactive static.

The group split into two camps: one wanted a "process" or therapeutic group so the members could model their behavior on the analyst's activity as he met each problem; the other wanted a technical seminar in which difficult cases could be discussed and resolved. Neither side would compromise. If someone brought in a problem with one of his groups, the "process" people would present their feelings toward the presenter and involve him in a personal interchange. If the "process" people got "stage center" with emotional communications, the "technical" camp would withdraw into a critical silence.

Even when these discrepancies were brought to the group's attention, no one demonstrated any willingness to give the other any empathic understanding.

The talk tended to get more and more superficial and uninvolved. There were occasional whimpers of dissatisfaction with the way the group was working, but no one was going to "cop out" for fear of what his colleagues, with whom he had daily or weekly work contact, might say about him "behind his back." At the same time, no one was eager to umpire so that all would "play ball" in the spirit of mutual endeavor. When occasionally a member would assume custodial responsibility to see that the group functioned as a

viable corporate body, he was apt to get the brunt of everyone's dissatisfaction.

The analyst's interventions had progressively less impact on the way things went. His references to the group
contract were turned aside, or the "blame" was fastened
onto a scapegoat or an external factor. Members had too
many agendas against each other to work together. The
analyst's comments about their lack of concern for each
other was given short shrift: "Why should I care about M.
when she is always finding fault with me?"

The analyst took a new tack. He asked the members how
things were going along in the real world, particularly in
their work. They replied with enthusiasm. He asked in what
specific ways were things better, and they enumerated an
impressive list. He agreed that they had certainly learned a
great deal if he compared this response with their initial
accounts of less than satisfactory functioning. In light of
these achievements he could see no reason for the group to
continue. It had served its purpose.

The intervention was met with silence. Then a member
asked about the difficulties they were experiencing at
present in the group. The analyst observed that working on
the immediate problems they were having among themselves did not seem to interest them. He could understand
that. After all, the real world was more important.

Several members became uneasy. What would induce
the analyst to keep the group going? He indicated that he
found cooperative groups more interesting. At this point, he
would not put this group in that category. There was little
incentive for him to work with them.

Members began to ask what was awry. The analyst countered by asking them what they thought made him dissatisfied with their functioning. When he would not play into
their ploy of denial and ignorance, the members began—
hesitantly and sometimes sheepishly—to spell out how they
avoided gelling as a group.

With this acknowledgment came a surprising sense of
despair and defeat. Many had found themselves competitive
as long as they could remember. How could they hope to
correct it? The analyst explained that this was not the immediate problem. What was needed now was active observation. They might watch themselves engaging in their

noncooperative behavior in the now, and do nothing about it but note it. Most important, they could begin to point out these deviations to each other.

It began to look as though the scales were tilting back toward a working equilibrium. The change was deceptive. The group began to change from rebellious adolescents into watchdogs. Members seemed to be out to catch each other in an uncooperative act. Each outdid the others in policing the group. Wearing this badge of righteous authority, it was a good way to express covert aggression.

If anyone talked about himself, he was brought to task. "You're being narcissistic again. What do you feel about us?" Outside or office difficulties were soon taboo.

If a member did not feel comfortable talking about how he experienced another member, his peers ignored his qualms. Treating the matter as if it were a peccadillo, they would put relentless pressure on the hapless member to reveal everything. This would only increase his reluctance, and what followed would be either an impasse with much bickering or an emotional outburst by the member. The analyst had to intervene time and again to control the "eager beavers" and open some interpersonal space around a harassed victim. For his efforts he was berated and attacked by the rest of the group. They contended that they were just doing their job.

The analyst acknowledged that they appeared to be cooperating because they were enforcing the contract. But the literal way of interpreting it made a mockery of their working agreement. Some members agreed with him and began a systematic attack on the more obvious culprits.

The analyst now interceded in their defense. No member was really to blame. After all, they were all knowledgable professionals and seemed to be eager "to get it together." He had been thinking that the fault might lie elsewhere. Was he perhaps proving inadequate to the task of conducting this training group? He seemed to be unable to get them to work harmoniously.

A vocal minority seconded his speculation. They had understood he was going to run a training group and deal with the difficult problems they encountered. From what they experienced it appeared he could not even conduct their own group. They did not know how he had come by his reputation. "If you're supposed to be as good as you lecture and you don't like what is happening, why don't you make the gears mesh, and stop harping on our hang-ups?"

The analyst answered that he was interested not in getting the group to work together, but in finding out why they did not do so. For example, they asked for suggestions, but if he gave them one they turned it into a travesty of its intent. It was his impression that they did not want him to have the satisfaction of leading a cooperative group—just as earlier they had not wanted to give their clinic director the pleasure of guiding a smoothly-functioning organization.

Confirmation came at once from one of the subgroup leaders. "It's like the way we used to treat the supervisors. It was suicidal then and it's suicidal now. We would rather not function in our own best interests than give you the reward of thinking you know more than we do. If you get a smoothly-running group, you get the credit, not us. It's crazy."

The analyst seized the transferential opportunity and carried it as far as he could. Why should it matter to them if he got pleasure from the accomplishment? What gave them the idea that conducting successful groups was his only source of gratification? If this was an "ego trip" for him, why had he earlier suggested disbanding the group?

Confronted with these conundrums and contradictions, they began to uncover their conflicts with authority and their ambivalent attitudes toward competence. A changed atmosphere became apparent when an argument broke out between two members who were jockeying for a supervisory position in the clinic. The other members started questioning why the two were so cantankerous and contrary. This querying spread to everyone in the group. Memories of adolescent revolt were disinterred, sibling conflicts recalled, and tales of battles with willful parents recapitulated. Some were mentioned and dropped; others were analyzed and interpreted; and a few were merely commented on by the members: "So what's the big deal today?" There was less concern with the past than with the present. An openness about the thoughts in the here-and-now tied together and supported their toxic operations and feelings.

The members began to be aware of the group analyst as a real person trying to facilitate their learning. They started to solicit from him the kind of material that could help them verbalize freely, and the group moved along smoothly. There was a conscious effort to see that all aspects of the group worked for them. The interpersonal climate turned salubrious. Spontaneous communications began to cover the key areas of their professional and personal lives, ranging from dreams and sex to technical interventions in the groups they were conducting.

Though the resistance to cooperation cropped up frequently, it was more an individual than a group affair. Only when the other members overlooked it did the analyst treat it as a shared problem.

## TERMINATION RESISTANCES

In discussing the resistances to termination, it is helpful to keep in mind that there are many ways the group experience can be successfully terminated.

### *The Two-Year Breaker*

First, there is the two-year breaker. The group can accomplish much with presenting symptoms in two years. Feeling better, freer, less hedged in by his symptomatology, a member may develop an urge to try it on his own. He finds he has other things to do with his spare time. This decision is neither opposed nor investigated verbally. His wish is respected. He is given the feeling that the group has no desire to hold on to him. One member summed up this attitude: "I know I can split and nobody is going to hassle me. I know, too, that if I need a little refueling, I can get back into the groove. And if I can't make it into this group, there will be another one."

Such a terminator may return in two to three years. By then he has tasted his newly acquired strengths, found some rewarding and some wanting. He has a definite sense of what it is like to be in group treatment and to be without it. When he comes back, it is with a determination to finish the task. It is no longer a matter of whether he will pop in or out.

This returner proves to be one of the group's most valuable mainstays. Less apt than others to put up with laxity or lack of therapeutic rigor, he instills a refreshing vitality in the process. He himself is excited by the return. As one member put it, "It feels like I was just on a needed vacation and, boy, am I glad to get back."

## The Plugger

Another type of terminator is the plugger. His symptoms have been ameliorated steadily. He no longer looks on himself as a social cripple. His taste of what he could become if he were to shed all "the excess baggage" has whetted his appetite for "the real work." Such a member enters what some professionals call the "middle phase."[4] He becomes a dependable participant who weaves the group into the fabric of his life. The meeting is a basic element of his weekly pattern. He would no more think of making other arrangements on his group night than he would consider changing his name or Social Security number. His investment in it is total. He gives the group fee the same priority as his rent or his income tax.

There are still many transferential vissicitudes, interspersed with arid plateaus, but through the slight turns of his perceptions—brought about by the interchanges, communications, and insights of his peers—reality begins to assume a different design. With this change in perception the member is able to reshape the pattern of his daily life. He enlarges his social circle to take in diverse syntonic personalities. In the place of a few interests or one compulsive drive, he finds a dozen dormant aptitudes. He enjoys turning them into skills. Even his peers find aspects of his behavior to approve. The newer members may admire his spontaneity, his ability to hear beyond the spoken word, his acceptance of their limitations, and his minimal preoccupation with himself.

The awareness that it is time to leave comes gradually. The member begins to look beyond the group to the wider world. He may aim at a change in his career, push for specialized education, apply for a promising position out of town, or chance on a rewarding relationship. Increasingly, it occupies more of his time.

New types of dreams may hint at what is coming. One member dreamed he was gathering the final pieces of equipment for an expedition into an undeveloped part of the world. Another reported making arrangements in his dream to move into a longed-for apartment overlooking the Hudson River. The group has no difficulty deciphering these communiqués from the unconscious.

The time finally comes with an announcement setting the date. In the weeks that remain, the member casts off the last strands of transferential connections. He becomes problem-centered and reality-oriented.

The final day may be one of elation, some separation anxiety, some bittersweet tears, and a final leave-taking with assurances to some members that they will see him again.

### The Turmoil Leaver

The third terminator is the turmoil leaver. For the initially more disturbed member, the road to freedom from treatment is more tortuous. Even making the decision to depart takes on the semblance of an internal tug-of-war. At one session, he is sailing off on a wave of confidence and independence; at the next, he is sunken into a depression and reports that the group's agreement has made him feel rejected. Members who told him he was ready to leave were just "soft-soaping" him. When the decision is "finalized," the matter is still not settled. The deviant behavior he discarded "once and for all" a year ago, returns with ravaging results. Even the original symptoms flare up with renewed intensity. Members are often baffled because they appear to arise from nowhere. In fact, they may see a battery of aberrations that they have never seen before. Contradictions pile up. The outgoing member may declare his decision null and void. The "one-man epidemic" he parades for exhibition should amply demonstrate to the members that he is in no condition to leave. In fact, he contends this would be the worst time for him to stop—he is sicker than ever before.

The regression turns into an attack on the group, the therapy, and the analyst. The treatment "did him no good"; it was a complete "flop"; he has not been helped at all. His job is in jeopardy; he has insomnia; his wife is "at him again"; and he is thinking of combining his treatment with hypnosis or massages. The analyst just wants to get rid of him to make way for an easier, wealthier, or more beautiful addition. He is going to stay until he is completely "put together."

This is no time for the analyst to get discouraged. If he understands the pattern of separation anxiety and the defense against it, what he is seeing is actually a positive sign. He works to resolve these revived resistances indirectly, asking the other members how they feel about the member's complaints. What is it all about?

A member who took a sunny stance about ending treatment became furious at the group just two weeks before terminating because the members would not take his problem with his sick dog seriously. He wanted no speculation that the dog might be himself. When the members persisted that he was overreacting—he had never discussed his dog before—he threatened suicide if anyone mentioned termination again. This irrational fury fell away when the analyst reminded him of his old tendency toward emotional intimidation, and a member pointed out that this threat represented an antiquated twist of his aggressive feelings.

Practically any resistance can reappear during the terminal phase, powered by the same ambivalence, doubts, and anxiety the member displayed earlier in treatment. Many a member gets too much secret gratification from his group membership, which he becomes aware of only when he is about to relinquish it. A member may feel guilty about being self-sufficient, in the belief that he does not deserve to be effective. One member went into a state of mourning because the end of his dependency on the group was equivalent to the death of his introjected mother.

Each such resistance has to be unmasked. Old ones entrenched in the character structure have to be worked through again and again. The analyst merely aids the group in recalling how previous attitudes or interventions worked with this member. It is ever a pleasant surprise how members can conjure up the appropriate things to say to the resistor, and in how short a period they are able to resolve these seemingly tenacious terminal obstacles.

As each reluctance is dissolved, signs of self-sufficiency reappear and with them thoughts of the future. The member reports handling outside problems successfully.

> A group did not accept the doubt a member worked up about her ability to work in the face of her returned depression. They provoked her into fights with them by insisting she could function at it with her "eyes closed." To the astonishment of all, at the end of one meeting she dropped the news that she had been promoted to be fashion editor of a large magazine. This did not stop her wavering, but her peers now kept a radar-like alertness for any hesitancy about her ability to "hack it alone." Each time they sensed it, she confirmed their intuition of her lurking fear that her sloughed-off symptoms would sneak back into her thoughts. They sensed it, and aired and dissipated it through group interchanges.

This is the time for immunization. Ideally, we would like to have the patient permanently free of his former disabilities and dependencies. There is a common belief that success in treatment rests in large part on a member's continued loyalty to and confidence in his group and his analyst, though he may never see either again. The feeling is that the ego of the preoedipal personality is too weak to tolerate dropping these props totally. He carries in his mind the picture of members, the analyst, or the feeling of the group support and clings to this mental matrix with the same trust as during his therapeutic years. In a crisis he draws on it: "What would H. do here?" If, under duress, this fails, he reverts to one of his obsolete symptoms.

The group analyst takes steps to see that there is minimal likelihood that this regression will occur or that there is any necessity to revive a relationship in fantasy to ballast one's shaky equilibrium. Using the feelings induced in him, the analyst returns the member's most feared expectations. Should the member have no sense of what the analyst is doing, and fall back into one of his antiquated defenses, more work is indicated. The rest of the members are frequently a background chorus. They pick up and echo in their own slang or style what the analyst is doing, and there is always a member who can do the analyst one better on the replaying. Using the same induction, peers feed the member toxoidal responses intuitively gauged to his mood and level until he demonstrates a desired permanent change of behavior.[3]

The sign that he is free of his old attitudes is seen when he recognizes that the interventions are playing back to him his own apprehensions. Either he does not respond to the "old record" or he may tell the group to stop it. When this occurs, he is considered more or less protected against a recurrence of his old symptoms. The resistant patterns have dissipated, rarely, if ever, to rear up again.

One member could not venture into any new endeavor without being overwhelmed by anxiety. Occupationally and socially, she considered herself a "quadraplegic"—totally immobilized. She expected to fail, to be revealed as a fake, or to make a fool of herself. She would demonstrate her panic by rigidly picking at the lint on her dress.

When she first entered group, she made no move toward anyone. If someone spoke to her, she would go through her lint-picking ritual. An aggressive actor took a sexual interest in her. This heightened her anxiety and her compulsion.

To get her to talk, her behavior was brought to her attention. Members began to remind her that she was not looking at them, that she was tightening up like a drumhead, "picking lint like daisies," hiding behind her blushing face. This behavior went on for months until it was traced to feelings of sexual inadequacy, and through persistent efforts of the members she began to talk to them. In about two years, she seemed to outgrow the pattern.

She began to take education courses at night and during her summer vacation signed up for a teaching program in a Vermont college, where she met an attentive teacher who was attracted by her beauty and withdrawn gentleness. In the fall he took a job in the city to be close to her. After much hesitation and encouragement from many quarters, she quit a copy-reading job and teamed up with her boy friend to open a nursery school. With considerable ingenuity they popularized it, and it flourished.

After four and a half years in group, and with much vacillation, she decided to terminate at the Christmas break. She was going to get married, and spend her honeymoon in Europe. There was some apprehension about the upcoming event, but she remained relatively calm through the fall. Her fiancé was very supportive and they were absorbed in the affairs of their school.

About two months before her departure, some members mentioned that they would miss her warmth and sweetness, but felt she was ready to go. They were certain things would work out for her without having the group. She tightened, blushed, lowered her head, and proceeded to pick at invisible pieces of thread on her dress.

The members could not get her to speak, and an uncomfortable but paralyzing pall settled over the group. The analyst asked the members if they thought she would make a botch of her wedding. After all, engagement is one thing and marriage is quite another. It really ties one in; no one can hide in an intimate relationship.

The member's hand stopped in mid-air. She whipped up her head and told him not to lose any sleep over it. She would manage quite well.

Another member chimed in: How did she know that? What made her think her husband wouldn't eventually see the anxious recluse behind that peaches-and-cream façade?

She retorted that if he did not know her now, he never would. And if the truth were known, it was she who kept *him* on an even keel.

Members marveled at the change in her once her dander was up. What would she have said if she had not resorted to picking at her skirt? She acknowledged she would have told them all that she loved them for what they had done for her and for what they were, but the thought had flashed in her head that she would sound ridiculous.

The analyst interjected that perhaps she could not afford that chance and maybe she would need the lint-picking routine the rest of her life when things got difficult.

She told him, "You will never see it again."

Once when a member mentioned her old fears, she reached for her lap with her fingers, looked at them, and burst out laughing instead. The mannerism was not seen again. During her last meeting with them she mentioned that the lint-searching was "gone for good." When she felt upset, she would "look it in the eye instead of looking away."

In the final moments there are vows to meet again on a social level after the "six-month period." This interval allows for the shedding of any transferential remnants. If there is any reality to the relationship, it will survive the break.

Sometimes a member arranges for an annual check-in to give the analyst a progress report. This kind of contact tapers off in time. The analyst may hear from the member through a referral, a marriage announcement, a news clipping, or a letter on the birth of a child, with pictures. Occasionally a member continues a year or so in individual treatment, as if it is a needed weaning period, seeing the private analyst at less frequent intervals as time goes on.

## *Initiated by the Analyst*

There is a fourth way to terminate group treatment. The analyst works on the obstacles to leave-taking long before the thought of termination occurs to the members. Since all the anxieties attendant to separation are resolved prior to that day, the termination itself does not present a problem. When the time arrives, the members are aware of their feelings and they part with the analyst and each other with only minimal difficulty.

> The executive director of a cottage residence, impressed by the results of his own group treatment, hit upon the idea of making the experience part of the in-training program of his junior staff members. He prevailed upon his former group analyst to accept a trial group.
>
> These junior staff people dealt with children and young adults who had been abandoned or were products of broken homes. They had been selected for their jobs because they could sympathize with their wards and had a particular zeal for their work. Much of their drive came from the fact they had had similar experiences in their own lives.
>
> Because of their deprived backgrounds, which early in the treatment came readily to the fore, the analyst realized that termination for any one of these members would present formidable obstacles. To make matters more complicated, the understanding between the executive director and the analyst was that it was to be a closed group that would terminate within two years.
>
> They plunged themselves into the group experience with an enthusiasm that was impressive. In spite of great bursts of aggression punctuated by plateaus of floundering, they amply demonstrated that they needed one another's

support, closeness, and understanding. This need generated a peculiarly difficult problem that led to the first termination resistance.

The residence set-up and the fact that they had similar therapeutic interests (almost all were social workers or psychologists-in-training) threw the members together in varied settings. When they experienced the initial exhilaration that came with verbalizing their feelings to each other, they did not restrict this activity to the group setting. They let their feelings spill out wherever they were, not only toward each other but toward others as well.

This freedom of communication led to chaotic confrontations with supervisors whom they were "leveling with," complaints from fellow workers who felt excluded by their "groupiness," and battles with their young charges at dinner tables. To the authorities it became questionable whether a therapy group was a viable training instrument in such an environment. The executive director called the analyst and told him he was under fire because the members were pouring out their feelings indiscriminately, rubbing superiors the wrong way, and in-grouping.

The analyst opened the following session by telling the members they were exhibiting their emotions after the sessions and this was not in the contract. The members resisted any discussion of their outside flagrancies, and insisted on sticking to the here-and-now. The analyst agreed that they were probably correct to live in the present, but since they had so many complicated contacts in their daily life, would the members be amenable to dispersing and spreading out through his other groups? They immediately opposed this suggestion. The analyst asked the most vociferous member what the hullaballoo was all about. Why don't the members just say goodbye to the group, calling it quits, and making this the last session? When they laid bare their objections, fears about family break-ups appeared. As the members tied these traumas to the group's possible dismemberment, the shared agitation settled down. In a calmer mood they began to investigate with the analyst why he was upset about their outside lives. Once the problem was clear to them, they agreed they had been too free between sessions, but they did not want to disband. They needed each other's help. The analyst asked if the members were willing to give up the pleasure of airing their feelings outside the sessions, in order to preserve the group as an entity. They agreed. By discussing their catastrophic expectations and relating these to their backgrounds, they unknowingly took the first step toward resolving resistances to termination.

The second terminal working-through was distinguished by the generalized interest the analyst displayed toward any separation incident. If a member mentioned breaking off a personal relationship, dropping a graduate course, or considering an "easier" job, the analyst would actively intervene: How would the member feel about dropping the group? Then he would draw the rest of the group's attention to the member's response.

A member related that he had dated the executive director's secretary, found her less than satisfactory, and, without giving the matter a second thought, dropped her. Under many pretexts she took to contacting him. When he was curt with her, she began to misplace messages for him, influenced the executive director against him, and generally made his life uncomfortable. All his peers agreed that it was a mistake to mix work and sex and let it go at that. The analyst wondered how they would feel if without warning this member stopped showing up in group and did not deign to mention it at work. The attitude toward the member changed. First the group found itself angry at him. The analyst wondered why. They revealed that they now identified with the girl. What did they care about her? Members began to talk about their own feelings of being abandoned. Incidents of being suddenly left or cut off from caring people cropped up. The analyst inquired how they would respond if he suddenly dropped them. The group's anxiety amplified. The analyst kept the group focused on investigating it until the constellation of feelings around loss of needed objects became less intense. For some members, the anxiety was ameliorated only when the analyst assured them that final leave-taking would be a mutual matter to be mutually discussed and agreed upon.

This reassurance proved to be a critical factor. No matter what uncertainty a member experienced after the announcement of a long break, such as the summer vacation, there was in the back of his mind the recognition that the analyst would return in September and the group would then reform. There would be no arbitrary severance. Because the relationship was not threatened by sudden and permanent rupture, separation anxieties could always be investigated with the cooperation of the conflict-free areas of a member's personality. Thus with minimal effort many difficulties were resolved.

The third termination resistance came at the end of the first year. The analyst gave the members a choice of tapering off the experience or continuing it. Without hesitation they chose the latter. For many the session was the "highlight of the week." But, to the analyst's surprise, his alternatives churned up annoyance in several members who had not demonstrated much of a relationship to him. These members had seemed to play down the importance of his presence. Singularly perceptive, they could weed out the chaff from the wheat in any crop of complaints without referring them to him. Now they were up in arms. Investigation revealed they were piqued at having exposed themselves in front of a person who seemed to care little for them. Their apprehensions, concealed until now, indicated that their fierce self-sufficiency was a reaction against feeling dependent.

One member described the pain he had felt when a Jesuit priest, who had taken an interest in him after his father had abandoned the family was suddenly transferred out of town. The news had reawakened the earlier parental trauma, and the member had sworn then never again to depend on anyone. Yet, much to his mortification, he found himself at the mercy of a person who could cut the interpersonal strings at will.

The members mutually penetrated each other's defenses against dependence feelings. There was much talk about how they protected themselves from becoming aware of them. Slowly, the realization sank in that to deny such emotions left them vulnerable and bereft. It was better to acknowledge the feelings and work with them than to ward them off.

Vacations provided opportunities to work through terminal resistances. Well in advance, the analyst would bring up the subject of taking a holiday. After setting the date, he would elicit the group's reactions. This announcement would lead to animated discussion, some members conceding that their feelings to his leaving were mixed. The stronger the transference, the greater the reaction. Many denied that the analyst's leaving had any importance. If there were no reactions to his announcement, that in itself would be investigated. Why did the members not care about his leaving?

During the second year, the analyst announced that he was taking two weeks' vacation over Thanksgiving, therefore, they would miss two sessions with him instead of the one he had indicated earlier.

One member objected vehemently: "These vacations are from hunger. You don't seem to give a damn about us."

The member was quickly joined by other members, who were equally sensitive to these ruptures: "You made a deal to meet us every week. Did the contract exclude the analyst?"

The analyst asked, "Well, shall I change my plans?"

This query mobilized the group's latent resentment.

"Absolutely! Cancel the vacation. No breaks without consulting us. If we are here, you be here!"

"What would you say if I told you the decisions about my personal life take top priority?"

This question provoked more emotional outbursts.

"You sound like a psychopath! You're not here for us, you're here for *you!*"

The analyst picked up on these tremors. First they were investigated as a total response. To the group as a whole he observed that the strong feelings about his plans were worth looking into. As these came to the fore in greater detail, he would select a member who had the strongest feeling the others could identify with and work with him. Then members were helped to look into the reactions of individual peers.

One member who was especially bitter was asked by a peer to explain to what he attributed the strength of his feelings.

"Tell you why I think this is cruddy. Our dear doctor is no better than my old man. It brings back the scenes in the family when my father would take off for the Catskills in the summer and Florida in the winter because that was where the money was for waiters. But would he take us along? Not on your life. During the summer there were no accommodations for his family at the resort. During the winter we had to stay in school and my mother had to take care of us. It brings back the fury I felt when I found out, ten years later, that all along he had one woman in the mountains and another at the beach. The bastard had one hell of a ball while we were lucky to be wearing decent shoes! Like our doctor, he led his own life and the world be damned."

His peers agreed that his grievance was legitimate. They joined him in venting their irritation and frustration at the analyst. With some difficulty, the analyst finally got them to look at the helplessness behind their rage.

Some members were not so outspoken. They tended to develop whatever physical symptoms they were wont to mobilize in the face of the loss of a treasured object. The discussion of these somatizations was given top priority in the meetings. What did the uneasiness in the member's stomach mean? If the headache could talk, what would come out?

Just around the holidays, even before the analyst mentioned leaving, one member would develop a rash on his neck and shoulders. This necessitated a trip on his doctor's advice to a hot, dry climate to clear up the condition under the sun. After the third sick leave, the analyst asked the group what it thought the "skin talk" meant. The member denied that it had any significance. But one of his peers wondered whether or not it was saying: "I am going to leave you before you leave me. And I've got a reason which is more valid than the one the analyst gave." This struck a responsive chord. The member's face broke into a smile. He told how, as a child, he would develop calculated colds and serious sprains. This enabled him to get what he wanted or helped him take control of situations. He had a recurrent fever which was guaranteed to draw his estranged father back to the home. The analyst pointed out that this member had grown more sophisticated over the years. Not only did he have the thought and the symptom, but he had managed to act on it to get the same gains as the party who offended him. Both the analyst and he were taking a vacation.

He had always known, in the shadowed recesses of his mind, that his body was communicating in a primitive manner. He consciously began to study his responses and became quite adept at deciphering the somatic communications of his peers.

The week of the analyst's departure, two members could be counted upon to whip up enthusiasm to meet without the leader. These alternate sessions were always as good as, and often better than, the sessions with the analyst. He would make it a point to congratulate them in their ability to function so well without him. Then he might ask how they would fare if they met without him for a month or six months. Perhaps they did not need him at all, if things went so well. The feeling behind each response was systematically probed.

Some members dealt with their anxiety by pressing the analyst to give them all his holiday dates and then making concurrent plans to take off work. Knowing what to expect gave them a feeling of control and order. But should the analyst suddenly announce that he would be away because of an unforeseen event, he was apt to create a generalized disturbance. If the suddenness of the leave-taking generated any sickness or death fantasies, the analyst would enlist the group's response to them until the feelings behind the fantasies were perceived and understood.

A significant step toward the resolution of termination-resistances occurred by chance. One day the group assembled at the analyst's office, and he did not appear. After waiting impatiently for fifteen minutes, a member went to a telephone booth and called the analyst's answering service. Sure enough, a message had been left: the analyst was unavoidably detained and would be a half-hour late. Concern began to mount.

When he arrived forty minutes later, many of the members were beside themselves with anxiety and fury. The bedlam shook the walls for ten minutes while the analyst said nothing. A subgroup leader finally silenced them and directed a question at the analyst.

"How come you say nothing?"

"Doesn't seem to me that anyone is in a listening frame of mind."

"We're listening!"

"Okay, I was late. What's all the fuss about? What did you think happened to me?"

The apprehension speculations ran in every direction.

"Who knows? You might have been crippled in an accident. Why didn't you call the director's office earlier?"

"You never did this before. By the end of ten minutes, I thought this is it, you're never coming back."

"I skipped over the feeling. My mind was clicking away on how to get a new leader—until I saw you. Then I got the picture of how mad I really was."

"First thing that hit me was that you were sick and you had to go to the hospital. Maybe you had a strep throat or something serious, like cancer."

These imaginative scripts for personal disaster and abandonment were rich and elaborate. Following the analyst's lead, the members took apart each other's expectations and traced them to their genetic roots. The wish element was separated from the historical base; the emotions behind the rage and trauma were uncovered and exposed.

There was no incident that was not exploited for its termination potential. One Friday the analyst mentioned that he would not be meeting the group the following week because his office would be painted on that day. The members took exception to this arrangement. Why didn't he deal with such matters on his vacation time? Why did he use their time? When their attacking questions were accepted without retaliation, the hue and cry subsided. A member suggested meeting in the executive director's conference room, which he was sure would be available on a Friday afternoon. The analyst wondered what was so special about having him present? Why not hold an alternate session?

By always presenting himself as a target or subject of discussion when there was any possibility of separation, he stimulated the emergence of a large range of attitudes, feelings, and memories.

By the end of the second year, all reactions to the analyst's vacations had lost their anxiety charge. There were few flare-ups of the old symptoms. In September he began to explore with the members how they would feel about finishing as a group by November. The members received the suggestion with comparative equanimity. There was a concerted effort to round out unfinished business. Core conflicts were reviewed; the functioning of each member was compared to that of his initial entry into the group; problems that had diminished but were still exerting toxic effects were highlighted; and where it seemed advisable, some members were encouraged to seek individual or further group treatment. But, generally, the idea of termination was transformed into the concept of graduation.

The session before the last was one of mixed emotions. There was some mourning about the disbanding of the group. There was also an expression of respect for the analyst, particularly for the way he had maintained his awareness of each member's idiosyncracies and needs, without losing grasp of what was happening to the group as a whole. The members then pressed him to reveal how *he* felt about closing the chapter on the group. The analyst told them frankly that he enjoyed working with them and they had every right to be proud of their personal and professional growth. He would miss them. If he permitted himself to be guided by his personal drive to help people grow into maturity, he might have extended the life of the group another year. But he had to weigh that alternative against the fact that he had made an agreement with the executive director to terminate the group within two years, keeping it thereby within the time-frame of their in-training program. He had found the members a constant challenge and they had taught him as much as any experience he had ever had.

In the interaction that followed, the final fragments of the resistance to termination faded away. One member described the sense of power the experience had given him. He had always taken a subservient attitude to his elders who he felt had the prescience of aged sages. In his mind, they knew what he could never seem to learn. What he had discovered in the group was that this was merely an illusion, a figment of his anxiety and frustration. He had watched others successfully challenge the analyst. It had given him the courage to confront men older than himself and he had found he could be their equal. As his sense of equality grew, so did his freedom to enjoy them and realistically appraise them, just as he now viewed the analyst as a person to respect, as well as one who had assets and limitations.

Other members echoed his objective appraisal of the analyst. They recalled incidents in which, as they developed greater trust and respect for each other, they had functioned without his help. They were fascinated by the idea that the group was greater than any of its members, yet it freed each of them to be his own person.

A member mentioned that since the next session would be the last one, he had a suggestion: They had met without the analyst only when he went on vacations. Why not meet without him now—knowing he was around—and see how things went? Let them see if this alternate was just a way of softening their anxiety at his leaving or whether they could use it fruitfully on their own. The idea was seized upon by the others. It was agreed that the night before the last session fitted into everyone's schedule.

The last session was a quiet one. It began with a verbally shared satisfaction about the way they had handled themselves and enjoyed the session of the previous night. Gone was any posture of gratitude for the experience. There were no expressions of indebtedness, but neither were there any grievances toward the analyst.

The general feeling was that the two years had had a great impact on their lives. There were questions. Some members were baffled by the fact that much of the change had occurred outside of their awareness. The analyst answered some of the questions. Then the rest decided that knowing or not knowing was unimportant. Did the baffled ones want the analyst to spend the rest of the last session giving them a rundown on the past? The matter was dropped.

Each time a member mentioned with regret that it was over, another member would say that it was not. They would be seeing each other every day and they could always call on each other.

One member noted that the one person they would not encounter in the halls would be the analyst. All turned to him, some with quiet smiles, some with tears. No one spoke for a few minutes. A member suggested that they were not saying goodbye to an experience; they were saying goodbye to a family, and it was really the head of the family that made a family feel its oneness. They might meet again without him, but somewhere on the fringes of their feelings he would always be with them. He guessed that they had taken him in, like a template, and much of what they did would be patterned after "how he would have done it," even when they did not know it. All spoke openly to him without anxiety or defensiveness.

At the end, they all shook his hand. Some murmured that they would write to him. Others put on a bravura cover of joviality that threatened to break down. A member kissed him on the cheek. The group left.

We have spelled out the five major group resistances: treatment-destructive, status quo, progress, teamwork, and terminal. One must not get fixed notions about their sequentiality. The analyst has to keep an open and flexible mind. The toxic treatment-destructive resistances can appear in the terminal period, and the resistances to cooperation can dominate the opening period. There is no immutable law governing the order of their appearance. The crucial factor is to always be ready to identify them when they appear, and to be willing to sit with them until a means of resolving them is devised. Timing and spontaneity are the key words here. One is not sacrificed for the other. With a good personal group analysis, a grasp of a body of theory, and adequate leader experience, the unconscious ego will deal in a creative way with most group obstacles to progressive communication.

# Chapter 7

# PREPARING THE GROUP FOR THE INDIVIDUAL

Inasmuch as conjoint analysis involves a number of different therapists and patients interacting and transacting directly and indirectly, our experience has forced us to think through quite carefully the procedures involved in preparing the group for the new member.[2] Unless the fantasies, anxieties, and expectations of the new member and his future colleagues are explored, discharged, and understood by all those involved, the group experience for all will not be as productive as possible.

It is virtually axiomatic in both the theory and practice of group psychotherapy and psychoanalysis that the advent of a newcomer activates a complex interpersonal situation.[3] For the group members, on whom we will focus exclusively in this section, memories, affects, and fantasies related to siblings and other competitors are stimulated, and ambivalent feelings towards parents are frequently reawakened or compounded. The therapeutic group, like all groups, requires of its members and therapist myriad adaptations at this time. Subgroups often become realigned, the parental surrogate has new demands placed upon him, and the members, usually without exception, are obliged to relate to everyone in the group within a changed emotional environment.[3]

The multiple transference phenomena that are stimulated and their expression depends, of course, on where the group is in its own unique development. If the group is at an oedipal level, then the new member will probably be experienced within that emotional constellation, i.e., the women will experience a new woman as a competitor and the men will probably compete with each other for her love and admiration. On the other hand, if the group is dealing with preoedipal themes and struggling for position with each other in order to get the group therapist's emotional nurturance, then there is a good chance that the new member will be experienced as a rival for the maternal breast.[2, 3]

The major task for the group therapist is to be sensitive as to where the group is psychosocially. With this understanding, he can help the members explore the meaning of the new member's entrance in terms of where they are in their own therapeutic development and resolve some of the conflicts that are related to where they are in their current maturation. In effect, the stage of the group's development will determine, in large part, the group's responses to the new member.

The first clinical illustration that we will present describes a group that had been working together for approximately three months. It was composed of individuals who had a lot of preoedipal difficulties, i.e., conflict in trusting others and anxiety in coping with aggressive fantasies. Several of the members had rather fragmented ego development, i.e., weaknesses in judgment, reality testing, and frustration tolerance. Furthermore, most of the members had previous therapeutic experiences that failed in the sense that the members left treatment prematurely, feeling they were misunderstood and that their therapeutic needs were not adequately or appropriately met.

During the three months that the group had been meeting, most of the discussion was dominated by the theme of the "enemy therapist." The therapist was characterized as being a selfish individual who was concerned with his own needs exclusively. A narcissistic figure, the "enemy therapist" used curious techniques to force people "to talk against their will," "was over concerned with money," and "didn't care about people's emotional hunger." While most of the references to the "enemy therapist" dealt with the members' previous therapeutic encounters, it was clear that the current group therapist was being tested and warned, for almost every member in his or her own unique manner was ventilating his distrust, disappointment, and discouragement with his or her previous therapy.

As the group members were more and more focusing on their current therapist, as they were more and more vying for his attention, as the theme of sharing became less latent, it was felt by the group therapist that an introduction of a new member would be timely. As has been reiterated, in conjoint analysis every therapeutic utterance or act is designed to meet and enhance maturational needs. It was felt that the introduction of the new member at this stage of the group's development would help the members direct their rage at the preoedipal mother therapist, reawaken suppressed and repressed memories and affects, and deal with past and present sibling rivalry and competition.

> At the 13th session, the group therapist started the session by saying, "There is the possibility of bringing in a new member. How do you feel about it?" Mike quickly replied, "O.K. by me." After a two minute silence, Roberta stated, "I would like to know more about him or her. Is it someone who couldn't get along with his therapist? Is he like one of

us?" Another silence. Zelda remarked, "Look we're one big happy family having a good time!" Several members nodded assent and then Moe said "That's why it's O.K. by me to have another member in the group. We'll have one more person to knock all of our therapists". Jerry turned to the group therapist and said, "How do you feel about it? Do you want another member?" The group therapist asked, "How do you think I feel about it? Do I want to increase the membership of this group?"

The group members then attacked the therapist. Moe said, "You pompous ass! You never answer questions. You are not only ungiving but you just want more money and more talk from us." Grace, Sally, and Mike took turns saying, "Right on!" "Bravo", and "Hurrah." Zelda recalled how she felt when her youngest brother was born. "I was out in the cold" and she began to weep. Other members recalled how they felt displaced by their siblings and how their parents did not understand their anger and feelings of impotent rage.

In the next several sessions, the group therapist was again badgered with angry statements. Further memories of being displaced in their own original families were recalled by the group members, but they slowly began to offer a lot of compassion to each other. With the release of their hostility, with memories of the past discharged, the members turned to empathize with the idea of a new member and his feelings. Said Roberta, "Hell, I wouldn't want to be stopped from having therapy. Why should I stop someone else!" Roberta's statement became the group's conviction.

In the above clinical illustration, we have an example of a group at a preoedipal stage. At first, when the idea of a newcomer is presented, defenses are erected against the expression of aggression, a very common phenomenon with patients who have severe conflicts at this level of maturation. However, when the group therapist frustrated one member by not stating his (the therapist's) own feelings, the aggressive fantasies toward the preoedipal mother were released. "You care about yourself only!" "You are not for us!" seem to be the predominant themes in the group.

When the group therapist does not retaliate but remains silent, the members are able to recall important memories and eventually move towards a partial acceptance of a new sibling. Through this experience, frustration tolerance becomes stronger and capacity for object relations becomes increased.

The following example is of a group at an oedipal stage. Members were examining their sexual feelings towards each other, were competing with other men for the admiration of the women, and the women were vying for the men's attention. The group analyst was experienced as an ideal father figure. The men felt very ambivalent towards him and the women competed for a favorable position vis-à-vis him. The following transpired at the group's 55th session:

Therapist: "I am planning to bring in a new member soon." (A 30-second silence) Bob asked: "Is it a male or female?" Therapist: "Why do you want to know?" Jim responded, "You've got to be the big shot and run the show, don't you?" Sally said to Jim, "Oh, Jim, you're a nice guy and all that but he (the therapist) knows what he's doing!" Bob and Jim attacked Sally for always defending the therapist and both asked her why she does not respect them the same way she does the group therapist. Sally laughed and said, "Because he's got a bigger penis!"

Bertha had a fantasy that the new member was really a baby that she and the therapist will mother and father. Several women members expressed their hostility and envy towards Bertha for her fantasy and eventually acknowledged that their thoughts and feelings were somewhat similar. The men denounce the therapist again. Sally turned to Jim and said, "You know, I could have a baby with you. It might be fun." Jim enjoyed Sally's fantasy but said that the group analyst will disapprove. Bob said, "He doesn't disapprove of thoughts—only 'acting out'!"

Several of the women members wondered if the new member will be a woman and voiced their worries about whether she will be more attractive than they. The men reassured the women, but then they started to consider what will they feel if the new member turns out to be a man. Again, the women reassure the men that they are safe!

At later sessions the group members recalled fantasies and memories from their childhood related to their parents' sexual lives. Some suggested that the group therapist had the best sex life in the world. Finally, at Barbara's suggestion that "we shouldn't be so eager to mother and father the new member because that may be our need and not his or hers," the group appeared ready to greet the new member.

These clinical examples indicate that although the two groups each have to cope with an identical task, namely, assimilating a new member into their midsts, their responses are very different. In the first example, the group is at a preoedipal level, consequently, the new member is perceived as a rival for the maternal breast and much more anger is directed at the group therapist. In the second example, the members are functioning on an oedipal level and the response to the new member has sexual and oedipal overtones. The members relate more to each other and several of them fantasy themselves as parental figures. In the second group the members can work towards taming their rivalrous feelings towards parents of the same sex and can get some understanding of their incestuous fantasies. After doing this, they are much more enabled to greet the member as he is, rather than as an embodiment of a fantasy.

In some ways the introduction of a new member into a group provokes a trauma for its members. Furthermore, the characteristic responses of the members may be likened to children's responses when they attempt to master anxiety through play. The introduction of a new member, regardless of where the group is in its maturational development, does induce some regression for the members.[1]

Introducing a patient into a group may be compared to introducing an infant to a family. How the group therapist uses himself should be how a mature parent handles himself throughout this important time.

To have a baby is the parents' decision. *They* plan for the child and only *they* can produce it. When conception takes place, they decide when to tell the rest of the family of *their* decision. They tell their children approximately when the baby is coming, but what he or she will be like, no one can foretell. The sex, the size, and the shape are mysteries. That the children are entitled to have a response is beyond question. They can and should fantasize what they would like or not like to have and express what the coming child means to them. Parents, in turn, have an obligation to prepare the children for the coming event, absorb their children's negative feelings and encourage their expression. But, it is the parents' baby and when it comes, family members need help in adapting to the newcomer and new roles, tasks, and assignments have to be considered and examined.

In the two clinical examples that we have reviewed, the birth process was utilized as our paradigm. The group therapist in both instances assumed the role of the parent who decides when and how the family should be emotionally prepared for the newcomer. He produced the child, but at which group session was *his* decision, not the group's. The group therapist, we feel, can tell the group members approximately which session the new member is coming, but precisely which one, should be a surprise. The group therapist does not announce the sex, shape, size, or personality type of the newcomer but welcomes fantasies about the newcomer and encourages the expression of feelings and wishes concerning the event.[3]

Because the group therapist wants to help members relive old traumas and master painful affects and memories he works with the group members' reactions to their perception of the event. When the newcomer arrives, the group analyst reassesses the group and attempts to understand how the group family is doing by determining who is the big brother, who is the displaced sibling, and who is the jealous child competing with the parent. He then determines how he will use himself so that the modified family can move up the maturational ladder.

In sum, although the model of the birth process is constantly kept in mind in introducing the new member, the therapist's use of himself has to be adapted to the development, transference, themes, and resistances of the group.

*Chapter 8*

# CONJOINT TREATMENT IN ACTION: JANE

In order to appreciate how conjoint analysis can stimulate maturation and enrich the psychosocial functioning of patients, we are presenting in this chapter, two clinical vignettes that will describe some of the processes that transpired in the conjoint treatment of Jane and of David (Chap. 9).

## PRESENTING PROBLEMS

Jane entered individual treatment at the age of 23. A tall, attractive high school teacher, Jane was acutely depressed, suffered from migraine headaches, insomnia, phobias, and frigidity. She had recently left a large Midwestern city where her family resided and felt guilty about "abandoning" her parents and siblings. She had frequent wishes to return home, but on the other side of her ambivalence she felt that she would be squelched and controlled if she did so. Perhaps what concerned Jane even more than the afore-mentioned problems was the fact that she had a lot of interpersonal conflict with men. She was quick to "fall in love" with a man, make him the most important object in the world, and then became dissatisfied with him when he could not anticipate her wishes and gratify her wants imme-diately. At the time she sought therapy, she had just termi-nated a relationship with a young man and was in a rather agitated depression.

## FAMILY

Jane's father was a prominent banker and a highly re-spected community leader. He was described by Jane as very handsome, bright, and very much of a lady's man. He seemed to have a rather strong erotic interest in Jane, and the patient recalled that often she and her father would dine together in glamorous restaurants, conduct long tête-à-têtes late into the night in her father's study, and in many ways were "silent lovers."

Her father had a rather tempestuous relationship with Jane's mother and there were several separations for short duration between the parents. During these times Jane maintained contact with her father and it was she who often persuaded him to return home.

In contrast to her memories of her father, Jane experi-enced her mother as a very critical, competitive woman who frequently demeaned Jane, referred to her as gawky and unsexual, and seemed to enjoy calling to Jane's attention how mediocre the latter was, particularly with the opposite sex. Furthermore, her mother very actively and openly re-sented Jane's relationship with her father and from time to time would take Jane to the same restaurant that her father ate lunch and not permit her father to join them.

Jane had an older brother and a younger sister. The

brother, Larry, three years Jane's senior, was her mother's favorite, and he seemed to have a sexualized relationship with her mother much like Jane did with her father. Larry and Jane had numerous power struggles while growing up and their mother usually sided with Larry while their father remained "neutral." Peggy, the younger sister was the family scapegoat and was much derided and hated by all of the family members. At a young age she was institutionalzed in a residential treatment center and remained there for a number of years. The family had several full time maids over the years and Jane loved them, relating to them as mother figures.

Jane had few friends but was always a superior student. She was well liked by the peers she did befriend, but described herself as a child and as a teen-ager as quite self-conscious and lacking in confidence. She seemed to relate reasonably well to teachers and other individuals in authority, and was usually quite compliant.

## DIAGNOSIS

After several interviews, Jane's problems could be assessed. She was suffering from a rather acute oedipal conflict and was actively pursuing and trying to gratify incestuous fantasies when with men. Because of her strong competition and hatred towards women, her depression, sexual anxiety, and other problems could be viewed as a masochistic self-punishment for her sexual wishes toward the father and concomitant murderous fantasies toward the mother.

With further work with Jane, we were able to recognize that in addition to her oedipal problems were fears of abandonment and separation anxiety. These preoedipal problems were related to her mutually ambivalent relationship with the mother that probably started at about two years of age when Jane began to show some interest in autonomy.

Despite Jane's difficulties she manifested many ego strengths. She showed the capacity for much empathy in object relations and manifested good judgment and reality testing most of the time. In addition, she was flexible in modifying defenses and also showed reasonably good frustration tolerance and impulse control. We felt that she could make good use of conjoint analysis because of her ability to look at herself in relationships. Furthermore, we felt that with her experience of having two parents at odds with each other, it would be quite therapeutic for her to experience two parental figures working together in her behalf.

## INDIVIDUAL TTREATMENT

Jane was seen three times a week in individual treatment and when she started group treatment a year later, the individual therapy was reduced to twice a week. When Jane first started her treatment she verbalized a great deal of guilt for being on her own in New York. She felt that she had no right to enjoy her job, her own apartment, and her social life. After all, her family needed her for them to get along. When her therapist did not respond to her ambivalence about being in New York City, but listened to her mixed feelings for a number of sessions, Jane turned to him for advice and asked him what she should do. When this request was turned back to Jane and she was asked why she could not make up her own mind, Jane became very furious with the therapist and told him he was inattentive and not comforting "and all you want to do is just analyze me."

In her first few dreams Jane would attempt to sit on the therapist's lap and he would rebuff her, or else, his wife would yell at her for Jane's seductiveness. Jane then recalled how she was her father's "special girl" and was angry at her therapist for not treating her the same way. After a few months of treatment she formed a rather strong negative transference, but while she was berating the therapist for not gratifying her incestuous wishes, her depression lifted, she reported excellent progress in her work, and became quite orgasmic in her sexual relations. "Somehow this treatment is working even though I hate you," was Jane's thoughtful exclamation after several months of individual therapy.

As Jane got more interested in sustained relationships with men, two major themes asserted themselves. Because of her incestuous wishes, she found herself dating men "as opposite as you (i.e., the therapist) as I can find" and two, she became interested in men who were involved with other women. What seemed to be occurring at this stage of treatment? She was keeping separate her tender feelings toward the father image from her erotic ones and gratifying the latter only with men that she perceived as quite different from the father-therapist. This way, she would not have to feel the full impact of her incestuous feelings toward the father. Furthermore, part of her interest in "men with other women" could be understood as well. Much of her sexual satisfaction was experienced by her as a triumph and victory over her mother, rather than genuine object-related love.

When Jane's resistance to feeling her erotic feelings toward the therapist was pointed out to her, she recalled memories and fantasies of trying to seduce her father. As these memories and fantasies were recalled, she began more and more to see the therapist as a perfect sexual object: an idealized father. Rather dramtically, Jane went into a "flight of health." Her job performance increased by leaps and bounds, her relationships with men became enormously pleasureful, and she was symptom-free.

The "flight into health" defended against strong feelings of hatred toward and fear of retaliation from her mother and mother-figures. As she began to enjoy her dates with men and experienced other successes in her life, she also transferred on to her individual male therapist some of her feelings toward and conflicts with her mother. "You are against my having a good time. You are jealous of me!" bellowed Jane.

It became quite clear that Jane wanted the "mother-therapist" to become jealous of her. She constantly pointed out to him that she was a better person than he. When her wish to hurt the therapist and make him jealous of her was interpreted to her, dreams and fantasies of the therapist and/or her own mother dying followed this interpretation. On Jane's being eventually able to see how much she wanted to destroy women and seduce father-figures, and when she recognized how her mother and father never worked together in her behalf, we felt it was time for her to start a group experience.

In her individual treatment, Jane initially raved about how great her group therapist was and how much she enjoyed the group members. "They tell me I'm terrific, but it has nothing to do with your treatment," she proudly told her therapist. "I bet you'd like to get me out of there because you feel so inadequate" Jane later remarked. When the therapist suggested to Jane that maybe she would like to just have group therapy alone, she laughed and said, "Don't you understand, I like coming here to put you down. I want you to suffer like my mother made me suffer."

As Jane began to see that her difficulty with men had more to do with defeating women than with the men themselves, she became more confident with men in the group and on the outside and focused in her individual treatment on her interactions with women. She was able to analyze in her individual treatment how her wish to show-off to other women in the group was more important than the interaction and pleasure she got with a man or men. Sometimes she tried to get her individual therapist to punish her for her pleasureful interaction with certain men in the group or with the group analyst. When the punishment was not forthcoming from her therapist she could slowly look more carefully at her relationship with her mother and mother figures, particularly with her own provocativeness in them.

Slowly Jane's oedipal struggle was completely brought into her group treatment and her preoedipal problems became more observable in her one-to-one treatment. Part of her expectation of punishment from her individual therapist was because she enjoyed "abandoning you and doing things that are none of your business." The wish to abandon her therapist and have him suffer was interpreted to her as doing to the therapist what she felt her mother did to her. Memories then followed of her mother going away from the house to parties and on vacations as were expressions of mutual hatred between mother and Jane at the time Jane was two and three years old.

As Jane reported a feeling of increased self-esteem and a deepened sense of identity as a woman coming from her group treatment, her ego became strong enough to observe, report on, and analyze her murderous feelings toward her mother and mother-therapist. Dreams of her therapist going up in smoke, becoming a skeleton, and dying of a heart attack were reported at this time. However, as more murderous rage was discharged and its historical roots analyzed, Jane slowly began to forgive her mother and be less paranoid with her therapist.

As Jane's preoedipal problems become resolved and as her oedipal conflict becomes less intense, it is anticipated that separation will be planned between her and her individual therapist. She will continue for a while longer in group treatment.

As was stated in our introductory chapters, and as will become clearer from our description of Jane's group treatment, conjoint analysis was helpful to Jane because: (1) she had two parental figures who were working together in her behalf instead of pitting themselves against each other; (2) as preoedipal dimensions of her character structure were related to in individual treatment, she was strengthened to work in group treatment on oedipal conflicts, with each of the treatment experiences aiding each other; and (3) as Jane's ego functions were bolstered through her interpersonal experiences in her group treatment, she was more able to focus on primary process material and other residues from deeper layers of her unconscious.

## GROUP TREATMENT

At first Jane hardly spoke, except to answer questions put to her by the other members. Toward the analyst she was shy and respectful. She gave the impression that she could be easily written off and the members ignored her. Indeed, though her individual analyst declared that Jane was profiting from observing other members and identifying with them, her group analyst did not discern much movement. But in the middle of the third month matters took a decided turn.

The group was in a state of resistance to teamwork. Each member was more interested in "doing his or her thing" than in working together. One of the few islands of interaction, however, was a developing relationship between Evelyn, a 45-year-old magazine editor, and Richard, a 22-year-old actor. Evelyn would help Richard any way she could. Acquainted with the theatrical world, she could tell him what agent he should contact, what shows were about to be cast, and give him other invaluable tips. She idealized Richard. In return, he constantly flattered her.

One session Richard was late. A man named Roger opened by recounting a dream in which Jane played a silent helpless role. When the analyst asked Jane what she thought the dream was saying, she started to give an insightful description of its dynamics.

Suddenly the door opened and Richard stood on the threshold. Ignoring the fact that he was late, he boomed out that he had great news. His ally, Evelyn, silenced everyone to hear it. Roger took offense at the interruption: he wanted Jane to be allowed to finish. Richard said he had not known that "Miss Docile had a tongue." Jane uncharacteristically retorted she had not known that gigolos had priority.

Verbal brickbats began to fly. Evelyn and Richard proceeded to tear into Jane. The other members were bewildered. Jane began to shrink into herself; and tears came into her eyes. The analyst intervened energetically, addressing the group at large: Since when was it allright for a member to be intimidated? When did that proviso enter the therapeutic contract?

In response, for the first time in weeks, the members pulled themselves together and began working as a team. First, they told Evelyn to stay out of the interchange between Jane and Richard since she had no legitimate role in it. Saved from further flank attacks, Jane could now counter Richard's sarcasm. She parried each one of his barbs with a capsuled description of himself, calling him vain, indifferent to others, self-indulgent, self-seeking, and interested only in being the cynosure of everyone's attention. She supported each point with evidence she had gleaned since her arrival. To Jane, her behavior was both frightening and thrilling. She felt she was in a new place. She had never told someone off this way before. Once she stopped and stared uncertainly at the analyst, picking up her activity only when several members began to second her words. Richard's veneer lost its sheen. Bending under group pressure, he agreed to examine his behavior. Before the meeting ended, a number of members expressed their admiration of Jane. She beamed in response.

At the following session a member asked Jane how she had managed to stand up against Richard and Evelyn. Jane said it had been a fluke. Of course, she had talked about doing something like this many times in private sessions. But ordinarily she would have crumbled under the assault. It reminded her, she said, of the fights she used to have with her brother. Halfway through them she would be shattered because her mother would join in against her. The difference at the last session was that the analyst, unlike her father, who had stood aside with pseudo-objectivity, took a hand in the matter. He and the members gave her a sense of support. She no longer felt she was left alone to stave off the wolves. This tracing of her personal history appeared to be necessary to help Jane resolve each of her difficulties as they unfolded in the group treatment.

To grateful Jane the analyst took center stage. For a while she was easily influenced by him. He could do no wrong. Even when he was directing his comments to someone else about a totally alien subject, Jane would garner something of value from them that applied to her. She was sure he was always working for her; his interventions were really shaped with her in mind.

In turn, the group analyst took on the role consistent with Jane's expectations of him. In the beginning he was as supportive as conditions permitted. He was her personal defender: Jane was blameless until all the facts were in. If a peer confronted Jane about her aloofness, the analyst would ask for specific details. This would force hasty fellow members to substantiate their accusations. If they were awry or unduly harsh, he would make it a point to side with Jane. If necessary, he would probe the accuser: What was the message behind the accusation? What was really being said?

Unless Jane personally requested information from him, he did not deal with her underlying neurotic structures. If she insisted, he would verbally recognize her conscious motives and ascribe her unconscious intentions to historical antecedents. Most of her difficulties were attributed to "inadequate training in childhood." He avoided ego confrontations and focused on bringing her pathological tendencies to the surface. When an interpretation seemed indicated, he would ask the members what they thought was behind Jane's words or actions. For the most part, Jane would take the partially exposed patterns to her individual sessions for further exploration and discussion.

Meanwhile, meeting at lunch, the two therapists would give each other a running report on developments. Gradually, they found they were working along parallel lines, each picking up a direction the other had spotted, and following it as far as his particular setting, time, and conditions allowed.

For instance, if Jane attacked her individual analyst in the group, the matter would be thrown open for shared discussion. Several members who were also seeing the same individual analyst would correct any distortions of reality. Some members would encourage her to pursue new lines of investigation with him; some would bolster her assertiveness. Others would provide alternative ways of looking at what was taking place in the one-to-one setting. Conversely, the group experience was never ignored in the individual setting. Denigrating statements about another member were instantly investigated. Had Jane expressed that opinion to the person concerned? If not, why not? In this way the individual analyst was able to resolve Jane's reluctance to bring into the group all the material that had to do with the developing relationships there. In short, the aim in both settings was to keep the channels of interpersonal communication open.

Jane's positive comments were given the same consideration. If she extolled the individual therapist, her peers might agree that he was a superior person. But what made him so much better than her group analyst? Behind these glowing appreciations of the individual analyst often lay a negative attitude toward the group analyst. Once Jane put such objections into words, she experienced the phallic pleasure of devaluating him. Then the reason for the rave reports about the individual therapist was ascertained.

Yet another factor that afforded therapeutic leverage was the separating of the two levels of her conflict: preoedipal and oedipal. (The preoedipal events are those which occur before the age of four or five.) Every group relationship was fraught with fragments of these early strivings.

In one instance, the group was instrumental in working through a preoedipal pattern. Geoffrey, an exuberant member, developed an inordinate fondness for Jane. But unless he said the right thing at the right time in the right way, she would sharply bring him into line, often shaming him in the process. For a while her restrictive responses snuffed out his spontaneity, he would twist himself into a pretzel to please her.

This uneasy state of affairs was upset by the entrance into the group of a woman who was soon enchanted by Geoffrey's flashes of wit. As affectionate bonds with this admiring member strengthened, Geoffrey's former ebullience returned in all its peacock brilliance. He was no longer willing to be stifled by Jane. Now, he resisted her, and his retorts to her fault-finding became sharp and cutting. The rest of the group was drawn into their conflict because of the time it consumed. At first Jane would not listen to what the members thought of the matter. She felt misunderstood and humiliated. A canny member acknowledged that Jane had a need to order her environment. As this member put it, Jane used such control to suppress her own anxiety. If she did not regulate others she might lose some inner hold on herself. He thought the group should give her room. In fact, he made the "outrageous" suggestion that she be given the liberty to control anyone she had to as long as necessary. Naturally, members took exception to this idea, regarding it totally out of line and a blatant indulgence of her aberration.

Nevertheless, after much debate they agreed to let Jane supervise an entire session. The analyst acquiesced. Faced with such carte blanche, she denied that this was ever her real intent. Members got her to agree to a compromise: she would look at and consider every controlling maneuver they uncovered. As members picked up her ploys, Jane's bewilderment turned first to recognition, and then to the freedom to laugh at her games. Further, members helped her piece together the historical remnants. Jane was trying to "toilet train" others on a sophisticated level, doing unto them what had been done unto her. She was soon adroit at spotting these remnants herself, and the anal ordering ceased.

Working through a primitive pattern in such detail is seldom accomplished in the group setting. The analysts found that Jane's preoedipal "patches" were more apt to be magnified, sustained, and resolved in the step-by-step fashion afforded by the one-to-one treatment setting. In contrast, oedipal conflicts (which occur between the ages of four to seven and involve three or more people) could be seen and steadily worked on in the group setting. Members would uncover these undercurrents and apprise Jane of them. However, for one reason or another, they were often not dealt with in sufficient detail. Sometimes Jane was inaccessible to her peers and too vulnerable to what the group analyst would say. Sometimes, the group could not give the problem enough time because another theme was dominating the scene, or because it was brought into focus at the end of the session. Jane would take the conflict to her individual session where it would be reviewed, particularized, and leisurely traced to its sources.

In the main, the shared setting seemed to supply the optimal conditions, space, character, and freedom to reawaken and work on this pivotal drama. When Jane settled

into the oedipal phase, she showed that she was more interested in murder than in love, and the object of her hate was
a member of her own sex. If a woman showed an interest
in a man, Jane would find herself taking an equal interest
in him. At its onset she saw nothing amiss in this concern,
but she could not explain the excitement it aroused in her
each time it occurred.

Then a new member, Jerry, entered the group, and
soon a new wrangle was created. Jane smiled knowingly
when she saw him and he was surprised to see her: they
taught at the same school. After some pleasantries over the
coincidence, the subject was dropped. Another member,
Melissa, found Jerry attractive and fascinating. Jerry began
to play a remarkable role in her dreams and sexual fantasies. Melissa became seismographically sensitive to his
moods and was able to put an intuitive finger on what Jerry
was feeling when he was out of touch with his emotions,
which was his chronic complaint. He began to take notice
of Melissa. She responded by arriving at the sessions attrac-
tively dressed, sitting opposite him, and seeing his side in
any argument.

With Jane's involvement the triangle became complete. As Melissa's interest in Jerry increased, so did Jane's.
If Melissa made a move toward Jerry, Jane could be de-
pended upon to make a more aggressive one. She would
wait out Melissa's perceptive best with Jerry's difficulties
and then encapsulate Jerry's dynamics in a brilliant sen-
tence or two. Her bon mots were not easy to forget. Jerry
would keep referring to them. They demonstrated an insight into him that beggared anything Melissa could muster. When it came to attire, Jane had independent means as
well as exquisite taste. No matter what Melissa wore, at the
following session she was outclassed by Jane.

This oneupmanship enraged Melissa, who in an alternate session accused Jane of stealing Jerry away. Jane
brushed aside this allegation and would have clung to her

conviction of coincidence had not Jerry sided with Melissa. He pointed out that before he entered the group Jane and he had had at best a nodding acquaintance.

The other members were surprised; they had thought the two had known each other well enough to be on speaking terms. Jerry said they had been casually introduced at a faculty meeting and, except for amenities, there had been no further communication between them. They were vocational acquaintances and emotional strangers, and Jerry had written Jane off as a "cold fish." But now she was all smiles and arm-waving when their paths crossed. Faced with this new array of facts, the members began to take an active interest in the change in Jane's behavior. Why had Jerry suddenly seemed so exciting to her? As usual, when confronted by something she could not explain Jane became tense and defensive. People often work side by side and stumble onto a new level of relationship when conditions change, she said. What was this new level? What conditions had changed? When Jane had no answer, a member suggested that she found him appealing because of Melissa's interest in him. Another member referred to other times when that tendency had appeared fleetingly. These observations only amplified Jane's anxiety; she clammed up.

The following day Jane had an individual session, and she opened it by telling how she had been upset by the group. The therapist began systematically to investigate what had happened. As she aired her reasons for interfering with Melissa and Jerry, she recalled a dream of the previous night.

She had been trying to telephone the analyst. His phone rang, but each time he picked it up the operator cut her off. Associating to the dream, she wondered whether the analyst was her father and the operator her jealous and competitive mother who wanted to cut her off from her father. She insisted that the analyst give his view. He agreed that her interpretation was a possibility. This concurrence relieved Jane. But how did this tie in with the group experience? It was clear to Jane. She was only repeating history: doing to Melissa what her mother had done to her. The real culprit was the mother who had set that model. Jane liked this view of the mother. It lowered her anxiety level, and she felt free to go on to other matters.

The next group session was less turbulent. When Melissa addressed Jerry, Jane did not interfere. She seemed to have better control of herself. A member remarked that she appeared to have come to terms with the problem. Jane said she had thought so herself, but she found that communication between Jerry and Melissa still unsettled her. She told what she had uncovered through the dream. A member suggested that the operator in the dream might be Jane; it might be Jane who was cutting the line, and it might also be Jane who was attracted to her father and considered her mother the rival.

Jane became thoughtful. It certainly fitted on one level. She had always been dimly aware of the tendency in herself to eliminate rivals. In fact, the matter had been discussed in her private sessions. But she had never seen the connection so clearly. She reported incidents that showed how it took place in her daily life.

Consciously, Jane dropped the cutting-out tendency. But on a subthreshold level it kept percolating. Every so often it would competitively boil over, and members would call it to her attention. She was always amenable to looking at what happened. She would take the group's observations to her private sessions where each nuance would be examined from every angle. The eruptions decreased in frequency and the sporadic spewing-forth lost its intensity. A cooperative attitude toward women began to appear.

Jane's ability to accept and digest her peers' confrontations suggested to the group analyst that she no longer required his total support. He could be more direct and interpretive.

Where she had previously played out the oedipal drama with her peers, Jane now focused her emotional sights on the group analyst. This last phase began innocuously. She seemed to be developing a healthy identification with him, but it was soon clear that there was more to it. She was engaged in acting on her positive feelings rather than putting them into words.

For example, Jane announced that she had "stumbled" onto the solution of handling her rambunctious students at school. She had converted her classes into group sessions. When the students found they could air their feelings and problems and gain some understanding in the process, their restlessness lessened and they could work productively.

This news was delivered as if it were a gift to the analyst, who was expected to discuss the dynamics involved. The analyst complied until the subject became tiresome and a member broke in to suggest that Jane arrange for an individual session with the leader. Other members seconded this idea. Offended, Jane sulked in silence.

At the next group session, she paradoxically blocked out the other members by trying to get the analyst to talk about what was going on in the group that prevented her talking to him. To Jane this seemed quite discriminatory. How many times had she sat silently while other members took his full attention? Several objected that they were not cut out when others communicated with the analyst, but that there was something excluding about Jane's tactic. What did she really want of the analyst?

These questions unlocked Jane's memories of intimate talks with her father about what they should do about her mother's behavior, a problem in the family. One member suggested that the talks had not been innocent, but actually a conspiring to do away with the mother. Another added that at present the group represented her mother and the analyst, her father, and Jane wanted to get rid of the group. That rang a bell with Jane. It evoked feelings and memories about her father that were charged as much with hate as with love. She was finally assembling all the disparate and confusing fragments that had robbed her of direction in life. A tremendous ambivalence was on the verge of being resolved.

When Jane's negative feelings toward her father burst forth, she concomitantly took a dim view of the group analyst. There followed a succession of convoluted interactions with him. First, it looked as though Jane was back to modeling herself on the analyst. On closer inspection, however, was outdoing him. Jane now displayed a knack of tactfully bringing an ignored, overlooked member back into the flow of the group current, just before the analyst could do it. She indulged in this maneuver at the expense of participating constructively in the group interchanges.

A number of members began to make disparaging comparisons between the analyst's taciturnity and Jane's perspicacity. Because of the need of a subgroup to mobilize and put into words its negative feelings about the group leader, Jane's pattern was not pursued. For a while she had a heyday, slyly hectoring the analyst about neglecting interpersonal nuances between members and showing him his oversights.

A member brought in a problem about her daughter who was dropping out of school. She addressed it directly to the analyst. He began to investigate it with her. In the middle of the third question, Jane interjected her view of the difficulty. With incisive insight, Jane explained all the dynamics involved to the baffled member. First the member was relieved, then awed by Jane's astuteness. She accused the leader of "peppering" her with questions instead of giving her the aid Jane did.

The analyst acknowledged that Jane was excelling him in sensitivity. But what was the meaning of Jane's sudden altruism? To what should they all attribute this remarkable change? When a few rivalrous comembers began to share their thoughts on the matter, they consensually discovered that Jane was acting in on the feelings of rejection she had experienced when the analyst did not energetically make room for her to be "alone" with him in the group setting. He had not taken care of her, so she was doing unto others what she wanted him to do unto her; she hoped he would learn by example. At the same time, she was scolding him.

When this paradigm bubble burst, Jane engaged in an oblique maneuver for attention. If a man showed an interest in her, she would respond to him warmly, encourage his involvement, and they would rush along to a dead end, each discontented with the other. At that point, Jane would turn to the analyst and ask him what was wrong. If the analyst turned the matter back to the group, she would accuse him of confusing her. He seemed to show an interest in her, but when she needed him, he abandoned her. Jane insisted on an answer. The members, especially the men, would interrupt her demand with the contention that they could help her as much as the analyst could. What was she after from him? Was she indirectly appealing for sexual information, veiled by an interest in "dynamics?" Why would she not let them help her? Jane would claim the analyst knew more about her, had more experience, had greater psychoanalytic education. The men would counter that what they had to offer was more to the moment: spontaneous response and their emotional sense of her.

These exchanges would degenerate into bickering. A member would declare at this point that Jane was up to her old trick: wipe out the group and capture the therapist for herself. If the analyst supported this observation, she dropped the stance. If she related the interaction to her history, it was an indication that she understood what had taken place. This would be accompanied by a slight depression and an unexplained hopelessness. Later the same pattern would reappear, costumed in some new interpersonal guise.

In one session, Jane finally managed to try everyone's patience to such an extent that the group exploded at her. After the analyst calmed the emotional waters, the members as a unit examined for the "twentieth time" what Jane wanted that caused her to create so much interpersonal frustration. They divined her incestuous strivings and managed to get her cooperation by showing that all her previous attempts to reach the analyst had had a sexual basis. They told her that what she claimed she only needed, she actually craved. But since it was forbidden to eliminate the group and seduce the analyst, Jane arranged to get the group to stop her from going in this direction. Yet intervention from an outside control only whetted her desires. It led to a restless drive. But the closer Jane came to the analyst, the more anxious she became. The more the group stopped her, the more depressed and despondent she grew.

What was Jane to do now? Members agreed that she was finding it difficult just to observe the pattern unfold and let her unconscious ego do the work. She was stuck. There was no way to go into action on her desires, nor was action desirable. They had no answer for her.

Again Jane turned to the analyst. He acknowledged that the group was thwarted. This was due to Jane's basic strength: her stick-to-it-iveness. At the moment her tenacity was at the service of her negative side instead of her positive self. Jane was singularly determined not to solve the dilemma by mutual agreement. Unless she could permit free expression by the women in the group, she would remain afraid of them. By binding them, she was binding herself. But she was not allowing the women freedom or allowing herself to be accepting of the men, the analyst, or the members as a unit.

The group had seen this same script replayed a dozen

times with different lines. As long as Jane wanted to kill the woman-mother she would be in an upset state. And as long as she wanted to have sex with the analyst-father she could not get off dead center and see her options. When Jane would be willing to accept the analyst as desirable and to give up her compulsion to sleep with him, she would also be willing to relinquish her murderous feelings toward the women. All her conflicts were of one piece. Once Jane accomplished that, she would be free to find an available man outside the group and work out a rewarding relation with him.

The explanation sank in. Jane's homicidal feelings became a living experience for her. Each time she felt like destroying a woman, she mentioned it and expanded on the reasons. Instead of operating to corral the analyst, she began to talk about her love feelings toward him.

More working through has yet to be done. Much of it, no doubt, will take place in Jane's individual sessions, which allow more scope, time, and space for voyaging through her fantasy world. But she is on the road to resolving her major obstacle to a fulfilled life. She has by now virtually established a place for herself in the real world that she never held before.

# Chapter 9

# CONJOINT TREATMENT IN ACTION:
# DAVID

## Presenting Problems

David entered conjoint treatment at the age of 36. A very tall, well-built man with a strikingly handsome appearance, David was acutely depressed, suffered from migraine headaches, insomnia, nightmares, temper tantra, and free floating anxiety. "I don't remember a day in the last ten years when I wasn't depressed," said David in his initial consultation with his individual therapist. Although he was a very successful salesman and a man with many artistic, intellectual, and athletic skills, he hated himself with enormous venom and spent much time either castigating himself or demeaning others either overtly or in fantasy.

Although David had tried various forms of psychotherapy prior to his contacts with us, he failed to derive any benefit from his therapeutic encounters. His failures in therapy paralleled his relationships with men and women. "If I get involved with somebody, somehow it always ends in a battle with no possibility of reconciliation," David remarked early in his treatment. Despite his success in his work, David continually longed for a life on a farm and occasionally would visit agricultural sites and cry as he silently conversed with the animals.

## FAMILY

David described his father as a man toward whom he had very mixed feelings. He was ashamed of his father for being a taxicab driver who had limited intellectual uptake. Furthermore, David experienced his father as "prissy," "effeminate," and wondered if "perhaps he was a latent homosexual." Nonetheless, "there was and is something about Dad's gentleness and quietness that I've always liked. I feel like hugging and kissing him but I've always been scared to do so," stated David.

In contrast to his father, David's mother was described by him as rather "regal," "attractive," "sexual," and "elegant." "She was the brains of the family and always demeaned my father for not making it," David pointed out. She had a close alliance with David and the interaction between David and his mother was very often tinged with erotic overtones. "She made me feel very special and superior to my father, brothers, and sister" David remarked very proudly rather early in treatment.

David was always a superior student in the Catholic parochial schools that he attended. The school personnel, like his parents, denounced sexuality and most forms of pleasure and rather early in life to the time we met him, David was enormously guilty when he enjoyed himself viscerally, sexually, or in almost any activity that was stimulating.

Over the years and into adulthood, David had no intimate relationships. Although a good student academically, he spent a lot of time reading, fishing, daydreaming, and experienced nature almost always by himself. He always longed for a chum but felt that he was too unpleasant a person to be with and tended to shun most interpersonal associations.

It was surprising to us that with his history and his essentially seclusive existence that he became a very successful salesman. However, in his fantasies he continually longed to be president of his organization and enjoyed (in fantasy) ruling, demeaning, and ordering others around.

## DIAGNOSIS

Because David found it quite easy to communicate with us, we were able to make a rather full and comprehensive diagnosis early in our contact with him. Stimulated by his mother who viewed him as "His Majesty the Prince," David throughout his life was striving and struggling valiantly to maintain this position. Whenever he did not experience the grandiose, omnipotent feeling that he so frequently received from his mother, his narcissism was punctured, and he coped with this psychological injury by attacking frustrating objects with temper tantra or other forms of derision.

Because of his unique position with his mother, David was in a very difficult position with his father and father figures in general. He experienced Father as a tender, warm and somewhat effeminate man who "was always kind to me." David, therefore, found it very difficult to reconcile his strong murderous feelings towards a father he wished to supplant with his warm, tender feelings towards his kind and considerate father. Consequently, David turned much of his aggression inward, felt depressed, and frequently had masochistic and homosexual fantasies.

Because David both wished to defeat and submit to

men he was forever in an ambivalent struggle either feeling angry, aggressive, and victorious or sullen, depressed, and a loser. This conflict carried itself into most of his interpersonal relationships where he experienced considerable rejection from both men and women. Men reacted to his overt and covert hostility and women reacted to his excessive demands.

Despite the acute ambivalent struggle that seemed to pervade much of David's functioning, he had many assets. His reality testing, judgment, creativity, and very high intelligence were ego functions that could be well utilized in treatment and had contributed to his vocational and educational successes.

We felt that David could make good use of conjoint treatment because he was quite introspective, eager to communicate, could look at his role in interpersonal difficulties, and was highly motivated to understand himself.

## INDIVIDUAL TREATMENT

Although David presented himself as a depressed loser in the initial stages of treatment and appeared quite submissive to his therapist, this was soon followed by a contemptuous reaction toward the therapist. As early as his third session he was ready to quit his individual therapy because he was quite sure that his therapist was a homosexual. He was confident that the therapist was a homosexual because he had heard that the therapist was an educator in a school of social work "and any man in social work must be a homosexual."

When David was asked why he objected to receiving help from one who might be a homosexual, he told the therapist that the latter might seduce him. Fantasies of fellatio and anal intercourse were what the therapist was feeling toward David and "that was awful." When the therapist attempted to subject himself to examination with David and asked the patient how he, the therapist, "got that way," David told his therapist that the latter probably identified with a weak father and had remained very weak since his childhood. He became more and more contemptuous towards the analyst criticizing his clothes, his voice, his mannerisms, and virtually everything about him.

By the 10th session of once a week therapy, David pointed out that for the first time in 10 years he was not feeling depressed, as a matter of fact he was feeling very good on the job, was enjoying himself sexually and he reported that in his therapy group he was not only asserting himself with the men but he was feeling quite amorous towards the women.

The "analytic honeymoon" did not last very long. By David's 13th session, he was feeling a very acute depression again and instead of demeaning the therapist was now telling him what a tremendous expert he was, and he was sorry that he could not make progress "with such a competent therapist." When the therapist wondered if there was not a connection between damning the therapist and his current depression, David was able to recognize how his past relationship with his father was being recapitulated in his transference relationship with the therapist. He remarked how he always liked "looking down" at his father but somehow he "couldn't keep it up." When the analyst made the interpretation that David was now punishing himself for his contemptuous feelings towards the therapist, David began to cry.

He recalled how he always wanted to hug his father but felt afraid. Many passive homosexual fantasies towards father and the therapist were discharged and again David felt by the 20th session a sense of well being. "I guess part of me loves you and my father and I've always been scared to admit it," David acknowledged.

As David's defenses against his homosexual fantasies

were loosened, the energy consumed in these defenses liberated some of his libido. He started making one good business deal after another and reported "making a killing" on several occasions. When the therapist called David's attention to his constant use of the word "killing," many phallic competitive dreams were then reported.

He described being a pilot of an airplane and "soaring higher and higher" only to meet up with another airplane with the therapist piloting it. The two engaged in verbal and physical battles with one or the other being subdued. When several dreams such as the one described were reported, the therapist asked David to associate to what the battle between him and the therapist was all about. David brought out strong competitive feelings and fantasies towards the therapist and argued that he wanted to have a bigger penis. He pointed out that he was taller than the therapist, probably made more money, and reported that he was feeling the same way towards his group therapist.

David went on to describe arguments he was having with his superiors at work and was getting himself hated and unpopular. When it became clear to the therapist that David was acting out part of his transference in therapy with his superiors, this was pointed out to him. The therapist said, "You are taking the battle with me and Lou to work. You want to fight with men and then lose!" David told the therapist that the latter was wrong. "You don't understand. These guys are just incompetent and they need to be put in their place." This was followed by criticisms of the therapist's Freudian orientation and that the therapist did not know what he was doing.

Although the acting out at work abated, David continued to criticize the therapist's "lack of know how." When the therapist interpreted that David was eager to put the therapist in his place, a place lower than David, and demean him as he had enjoyed feeling towards his father, David began to have oedipal fantasies involving his mother.

David recalled how his mother loved him more than anybody else and presented one vignette after another describing how he was mother's "one and only." Although David enjoyed his special position, particularly vis-à-vis his siblings, he resented what he termed the "responsibility." Analysis of his associations to the "responsibility" revealed that as a boy he felt strong feelings of inadequacy with his mother when comparing himself to his father. To cope with uncomfortable feelings of guilt, inadequacy, and discomfort as father's rival, David also had wishes to submit to father.

During his 10th month of individual therapy David began to actively relive his latent homosexual wishes in the transference. Although coupled with defensive hostility, David began to report dreams and fantasies of sucking the analyst's penis, having anal intercourse with each other, and kissing each other. When David saw how these fantasies were usually followed by feeling contempt toward the analyst, he was able to see how he warded off tender feelings towards men by fighting with them. When "the fighting" defense was less needed, David reported that he was fighting less with his peers in his group therapy and also fighting less with his colleagues and superiors on his job. As a matter of fact when he realized more and more the defensive nature of his arguing and bickering and started to permit himself to feel more tender and loving, he became so popular at his company that he was offered the position of vice-president.

With the discharge of homosexual fantasies in the transference relationship, David more and more realized that in many ways he loved his father but identified with his mother's contempt towards him. He began to have more friends, became less compulsive in his living habits, and began to enjoy the theater, music, ballet, nature, and other ventures where he did not have to be a "superman."

As of this writing David is still in conjoint treatment.

In his individual analysis he is talking more and more about his group therapy experience thus demonstrating his increased capacity for interpersonal relationships as well as an assumption of more responsibility for his interpersonal difficulties. Although David can still regress to depressive bouts where his oedipal and homosexual conflicts erupt, there is no doubt that the year of conjoint treatment has interrupted a very ingrained pathological process. He shows more sustained love and concern for others, and he no longer suffers from migraine headaches, insomnia, and from the other symptoms that brought him into treatment.

## GROUP TREATMENT

When David entered the group the members were bickering over such diversionary details as whether they should meet the week before Christmas. David was fascinated by the way the analyst worked on the members' reluctances to face their negative feelings toward each other. He would nod in emphatic agreement whenever the analyst described another member's evasive behavior. He would eagerly support, echo, and occasionally enlarge on the leader's comments. In short, David seemed enthusiastically on the side of the authority figure.

To his private analyst, however, David painted a different picture. The group leader, he confided, was disorganized and "unable to pull it together." David said that if he were trained he could do a better job. He began to wonder how much training one really needed; the more he thought about it, the more he yearned to try his hand at the job.

As the individual analyst gradually resolved David's reluctance to speak up in the group, David began to openly challenge the group leader: "Do you really mean that?" . . . "Isn't there a simpler explanation?" When David's provocative attitude toward the leader was questioned by another member, he would be evasive: "Do I have to agree with *everything* he says?" But there was almost nothing the leader said with which David agreed.

The incident that crystallized David's negative attitude was a harmless joke told by another member:

> In the spirit of detente, the Soviets requested a translation of the Bible. A computer was programmed to do the job. A programmer fed into it the proverb, "The Spirit is willing but the Flesh is weak." It was translated into Russian and then, as a double-check, the programmer had it turned back into English. What came out was: "That Vodka is strong but the Meat is uncooked."

Several members chuckled and the analyst joined in. To everyone's surprise, David took umbrage at the group, and in particular, at the leader. He saw the joke as a gibe at himself and at the computer industry for which he worked. The group analyst, David charged, thought the business world was peopled with hollow humanoids. Several members told David he was "coming off the wall." This opinion only intensified David's paranoia. He demanded to know why the leader turned the others against him and why the leader hated him. When the analyst accepted the projection and asked why he should *not* be hated, David countered, "I'm a nice guy. I don't mean you any harm. If you hate me, that's your problem."

A member suggested that David was turning the facts upside down: it was not the analyst who hated David, but David who hated the analyst. With vehement denials, David called members who agreed with this view "brainwashed patsies." Further comments, no matter how helpfully intended, only incensed him. In sum, the group's efforts to help David understand himself were of little avail. As far as David was concerned, he was a victim of the leader's machinations.

A few sessions later the group leader entered the room to find David sitting in his chair. Defiantly, David asked him, "What are you going to do about it?" The analyst asked the members what his options were. Eddie, a forceful member, was all for dumping David out of the chair. But Sandra, a usually silent woman, thought David should have a chance to show what he could do. A number of members agreed. It was clear that David was expressing a shared resistance: many members preferred to do away with the leader rather than talk about their murderous impulses, and David was acting out their rebellious fantasies. The analyst, joining this resistance, took another seat.

At first, David liked the feel of the large chair. He sat upright, alert, took an active role in the interchanges. He offered a few insightful comments. But gaps appeared which he could not effectively bridge to keep the group interaction flowing. As David's effectiveness waned and members began to lose interest in him, he became fidgety. Moreover, David's symbolic seizure of authority made him equally uncomfortable. Every so often he would turn to the analyst to ask how he felt about having his chair usurped. When the analyst inquired as to how he *should* feel, David flared up at him for not soothing his guilt feelings.

David's sovereignty finally turned into a charade when he gave an inappropriate interpretation of one woman's anxiety; it had more to do with his own turmoil than hers. The woman turned to the group leader, but the latter only shrugged and nodded in David's direction. Cornered, David admitted his inability to help her. Two more perceptive members stepped in and clarified the woman's predicament for her.

To see others succeed where he had failed was almost more than David could take. Eddie twisted the knife with, "Better luck next time, Dr. Freud." Muttering "the hell with it," David dropped into another seat.

Members now expected the analyst to zero in on David's breach of custom with devastating detail. But the leader was too aware of David's humiliation. Instead, he admired David's enterprise; David had indirectly communicated important information about himself. The analyst's only reservation was that David had chosen to act on his feelings—impulsively to seize the chair, rather than to talk about the impulse.

The analyst then helped the members track down and reconstruct for David the drama he had been enacting. As a child, David had felt he could do a better job than his father, now he was sure he could make a better analyst than the group leader. Plumbing their own latent wishes that had led them to support David when he took over the analyst's chair, the members correctly divined that on a deeper level David wanted to do more than supplant the leader: He wanted to kill him.

David agreed with this view. But for him the immediate trauma of the experience was the discovery that he lacked the rigor, experience, and knowledge required for the job that had looked so easy. Sandra responded to his despair. Why, she asked, did he expect to accomplish in 20 minutes what it had taken the leader 20 years to achieve? David blurted out that even in that long a time he would not be able to do the job. Another member asked how David expected to succeed by imitation, by being more like someone else than being himself. Eddie added to David's mortification by observing that only a "jerk" would pay a professional and then try to do his work for him.

The analyst came to David's support. David had the right to try out any role he saw fit, and if he wanted to use his time in this kind of rehearsing, why should members object? Surprisingly, it was David who disagreed. The members were right, he said. He just could not stop showing people he could do things better. Sandra suggested that perhaps David was trying to prove he was unlike his weak father. The insight struck a chord. Tears rolled down

David's cheeks. To the hushed group he told of his humiliation when he had gotten on a bus with a group of high-school friends and found his father collecting fares. David swore he would never be put in that degrading position. He was going to own the company and hire men to collect fares or do menial work.

Sandra doubted whether the analyst or anyone in the room could be the crackerjack salesman David was. All he had to do, she said, was to be himself. However, David moaned: "And who is that?" The group gave David a picture of how they assessed both his strengths and shortcomings. As David began to partially accept this objective view of himself, he was also able to recall his mother's way of demeaning his father. He had assumed her attitude was right. But since on a deeper level David identified with his father, he took this same contemptuous attitude toward himself.

A test of David's new relation to authority followed his group experience when the sales manager's job opened up in his firm. But instead of offering it to David, the president hired an outsider. David accepted the blow with resignation and depression: He was probably not the type to take command; if the truth were faced, the job called for a more "dynamic operator."

When the group members tried to make him aware of this defense against his rage, David talked about going to some underdeveloped nation where his talents would be appreciated. It looked as if the group was getting nowhere until Eddie, with one of his usual bursts of exasperation, said that David's boss was probably right. David countered that the "bastard" was *never* right. The president was too power-hungry and calloused; he ran the company with a minimum of efficiency and a maximum of nepotism. Given half a chance, David said, he could do twice the job. The more he came in touch with his fury, the more he began to develop a plan to confront the president. He would pose a series of questions at a special board meeting that would expose the president's incompetence, get him kicked out.

Sandra pointed out that since it had not been helpful to David to try to unseat the analyst, how would it be to his advantage to try to unseat the president? Wouldn't he only be repeating himself? Wasn't there some other option open? Instead of withdrawing into silence, David listened intently as members spelled out a more cooperative attitude.

Over the next few sessions David reported he was devoting his energies to developing new sales ideas. The group encouraged him to bring them into the sessions. With the group's guidance he began to focus more on his work and less on the president's flaws. Several members showed him how he could best present his plan to the administration. Eventually, David's firm gave him the chance to head a sales campaign which proved singularly successful. David then began to speak admiringly of the president's leadership and admire his creative imagination.

With the waning of the intensity of David's drive to eliminate the group leader, another theme took over. Earlier in the group experience, David felt he had to watch his step with certain peers. He was particularly wary of Eddie, who freely attacked anyone who angered him. At this juncture Eddie was concerned about his own reluctance to leave the uncertain clothing industry and join his father's company as a partner. The move would give him financial freedom and a secure future. But Eddie avoided this decision most of his adult life because he did not feel competent enough to deal with his imperious parent.

David understood Eddie's struggle, but it irked him to see anyone using the group more effectively than himself. Eddie's growth became particularly challenging because David was just beginning to test his own strengths with his group siblings.

To his individual analyst, David criticized everything

Eddie said; but in the group he held his tongue to avoid Eddie's quick temper. Finally, unable to contain himself, David leaped to the defense of a woman over whom Eddie was riding roughshod. Eddie, he said, was no better than the imperious father he dreaded. Where did he get off finding fault with anyone, when he had so many flaws of his own?

Eddie returned David's criticisms with a vengeance. But David countered each thrust with a well-rehearsed insight into Eddie's character structure. Eddie finally resorted to invectives: "Let's face it, you always were a fucking coward. You need the excuse of a woman in distress to stand up to me." The truth hurt; David fell silent. Eddie kept enumerating David's weaknesses. The tension paralyzed the group. The leader intervened, asking why nobody was helping David find his tongue.

This broke the tension enough for some members to come to David's aid. One pointed out David was under no obligation to believe everything he heard. Another said David did not need to use somebody else's opinion to wipe himself out. Sandra praised David as the only group member to come to the defense of the troubled woman. David was heartened by the group support. He spent his individual sessions going over and over the incident, searching for weak links in the chain of Eddie's verbal invectives.

The next time Eddie delivered one of his roundhouse swings, David heard him out impassively and then hit back —hard. Eddie, he said to the members, was violating the group contract. No one had the right to jump on members. Did they want such a person in the group? Perhaps Eddie should be asked to leave. By the time Eddie recovered from this astounding proposal, David was more than ready for him: Was Eddie ever informed that members were not supposed to use four-letter words, that the group was not a place for character assasination? Eddie could do no more than apologize: He was just blowing off steam. David pressed his advantage: Cursing was no better than acting-out. Eddie had contracted to *talk* about his feelings, not throw verbal dung! It was a great victory for David. Members congratulated him on saying so well what he had to say, and though Eddie said nothing, he had a look of rage on his face. The battle lines were truly drawn.

Thereafter, whenever Eddie tried to "educate" a member, David would show the flaw was in the teacher rather than the pupil. The constant clashes were struggles for supremacy. If momentarily halted by one of Eddie's vicious quips, David could recover by uttering disarmingly: "I don't know how I feel about you, but it's not good." Artless candor in the heat of battle won David allies. Members began to "sit on" Eddie when he counterattacked. David was grateful for the help of his friends. He was particularly appreciative of the group analyst. David felt that the analyst gave him the "space" to work out his own way of dealing with an opponent.

The acceptance his new-found friends accorded David embarrassed him. He had difficulty acknowledging his growing feelings of affection for them. When the group analyst pointed out that he had such feelings, David squirmed in silence. In his individual sessions, he felt freer to verbalize these positive responses to his fellow members. But he still felt he would make a fool of himself if he babbled out "sentimental nothings." The compromise David reached was to deal with his positive feelings on the level of respect. He fastened on to a relatively quiet member whose academic achievements he admired. The other man also found merit in David's accomplishments, particularly when David described how he ingeniously surmounted a difficult language barrier to close a half-million-dollar, computer service contract with foreign clients. The two engaged in a number of respectful exchanges.

But as David felt warmer towards the man, he also became alarmed: He began to suspect the man of homosexual impulses. The man was puzzled. As far as he knew, he was not making any sexual overtures. This denial only fed fuel to David's suspicions. He finally accused the man of being a "closet queen." The group wanted to know how David reached his conclusion. When he claimed it was a matter of feeling, Eddie taunted him for being the "idiot irrational." Unable this time to muster any face-saving humor, David withdrew into one of his humiliated silences.

As usual, Sandra sensed the true state of affairs. After checking with David to make sure this experience had occurred to him before, she suggested that his old mechanism of projection was operating, and that the homosexual feelings really emanated from *him.* And what was so bad about that? Why did David have to deny these feelings? Members discovered that David equated *having* a feeling with *acting* on it, the very thing he accused Eddie of doing. Several members explained, in different ways, that David could *feel* any emotion and yet not be propelled into *doing* something. In fact, as long as David held on to the idea that feelings necessarily lead to action he would remain homophobic. He would be unable to convert the energy inherent in his primitive sexual feelings into genuine male friendships. He would have to live the life of a loner. Eventually, David accepted this understanding. As members kept focusing on David's tendency to imbue another person with his own feelings, the sexualization of David's male relationships diminished. He became less competitive with the other men in the group. A number of weeks later, David reported he was having enjoyable lunches with his co-workers, people he had avoided in and out of work hours.

David had long been fluctuating between idealizing, avoiding, and demeaning the women in the group. His declared approach was to test women out before he got involved. Yet, so far, he had sidestepped any such involvement within the therapeutic circle. Only Sandra showed any semblance of consistent interest in David, but even she admitted she was wasting her time lavishing attention on him. David was astonished by this statement. He acted as if he were unaware of her efforts. The group refreshed his memory.

Confused, David asked Sandra what she saw in him. She said that at times he could be kind, gentle, and loving. Visibly touched, David stumbled over his words. On the one hand, he was grateful she had seen something so hidden, yet so essential in him. On the other hand, he felt vulnerable and embarrassed that this aspect of his nature had been exposed. To hide his discomfort, David became aggressively skeptical of Sandra's concern. He enlarged on his philosophy of women, the gist of which was that a man never knows where he stands, and he should always be on his guard.

One of the women said: "In plain English, you don't trust us!" The rest of the women closed ranks in an indignant attack on David. Was all his recent courtesy and consideration for them just a maneuver to gain allies for his fight with Eddie? Was he merely an oily diplomat? David began to stutter, became agitated, and then fell silent.

The analyst pointed out that the women had formed a posse, and asked how it could help to gang up on David. Several men came to David's aid. With their help the pieces fell into place. David seemed unable to let himself experience love feelings; he was convinced he could not feel nor care for anyone. Why, therefore, should he try? A woman he had previously described as having "style and class" reminded him of a warm exchange they had earlier in the session. He agreed he had felt warmly then, but only for a moment. He added, "What is a moment in a lifetime?" The women were up in arms again. They accused David of wiping out any trace he could find of the caring part of his nature. Some saw in him characteristics of their husbands, and he became the brunt of transferential frustration.

The individual sessions became the only place now

where David could freely explore his discordant attitudes toward women. He discovered that he really wanted women to read his mind, to respond to his unspoken wishes with perfect comprehension. He resented having to make his wants known. Only if he received this mystical understanding from a woman without having to expend any effort, would romance be possible. It was true, he admitted, that Sandra may have sensed his needs. But he was not aware of these needs; therefore, he had no idea what she was doing and it was only natural that he should discount her efforts. Conversely, if David knew his needs but had to ask a woman to meet them, she took on the status of a servant, someone to be used and discarded.

With this understanding David began to respond to the women in a new way. Alice, a woman in the group who had written him off as incorrigible, now found herself attracted to David because of his awakened sensitivity. They fantasized themselves going across the country together. But Alice sensed a reserve in David even as they talked. David acknowledged that what she had told him made him feel good, but he was afraid that the feeling was going to go away and that he would not like her later.

How could David "let go" not knowing the outcome? He revealed that a protracted period of intimacy was a rare event in his life, and for good reason. He feared his own warmth because it would result in entrapment. Love, for David, foreshadowed the imprisonment of marriage. Alice urged him to live in the moment, to let the future write its own script. David flashed her an understanding smile. They resumed their fantasy-odyssey.

David is forming new types of relationships through his group interchanges. His bursts of criticism are less frequent. He is still argumentative, but there are longer interludes of friendliness. His withdrawals into silence have diminished and his projecting tendency has melted away.

Instead of trying to provoke his former peer–antagonists, David can at times express concern for their difficulties and be singularly helpful. He still has problems with the women in the group. But at least his doubts about them are in the open.

How is the efficacy of conjoint treatment demonstrated in the case of David? It could be argued that David might have done equally as well in combined treatment with the same therapist, or in either treatment modality alone. But in the authors' view, it is doubtful that anything other than this dual approach could have afforded such a precise delving into David's personality. In fact, the authors know of no method that could have permitted them to see separate elements of the same person with such clarity, and piece them together so productively.

During many discussions with the individual analyst, for instance, the group leader would be startled to hear that David was working on a vector of his life of which the group leader had no inkling. At times he wondered if the two analysts were not discussing two different people. The discrepancy was widest during the period that David felt contemptuous of his group therapist. He gave the individual analyst the impression that this critical attitude was out in the open in the group, keeping the private therapist in the dark on how he concealed his contempt from the leader. At the same time, David kept the group leader and his co-members in the dark about ideas to which he gave central emphasis in his individual sessions. For example, he told the individual therapist about plans to leave the city permanently, to head a company elsewhere. But he never mentioned this possibility in the group.

When the two therapists became alerted to the compartmentalization of material, they decided to inquire regularly whether attitudes mentioned in one setting had been brought up for discussion in the other. For instance, during one private hour David mentioned that the group analyst's ideas were not worth a wooden nickel. When the individual therapist asked him if he had aired this opinion in the group, David said he had not and would not. What was more, he was not going to discuss that issue again.

From then on, each time David alluded to his disdain of the group leader, the analyst investigated his attitude. David realized he could elicit comments from the usually taciturn private analyst by talking at great length about his disrespect for the group leader. Soon they could investigate why there was no carryover from one setting to the other.

This separation of arenas had positive value. David could turn his tendency to isolate emotional states to advantage. He could express rage where it was not dangerous, and deliver denunciations in comparative safety. There would be no retribution if he cursed his group analyst to the individual one.

But the split of functions was also valuable for the analysts—both in gathering information quickly and in ameliorating David's tendency to act out. They could pick up patterns that became apparent in one setting, but were still latent in sessions with the other therapist. Together, they could predict and control the intensity of David's resistances. For example, David began to talk in his individual sessions about his idealization of women but did not mention it in the group. As David saw it, all his relationships with women were doomed on many levels. In particular, he felt he had to mistreat every one he put up on a pedestal. Only when he degraded his adored object, could he relate to her as an equal. But by then, he found he had "goofed it." Knowing this, the therapists set about to work out a prophylactic prediction to alert David to his unconscious script. Thus, when David began to describe Adele, a new group member, to his individual therapist in idealized language, he was warned he was going to abuse her. Adele was told by the group leader that David's sincere expression of love feelings would soon be followed by his infantile hate. This effectively insulated Adele against David's later tirades. Meanwhile, each time David praised Adele the warning was repeated in both his treatment settings with the exact words shaped to fit the specific situation. This intervention successfully curtailed David's destructive degrading and helped him to uncover his lack of self-worth vis-à-vis any woman he admired.

There was still another factor in this segregation of analytic themes. David never devoted sustained energy to any task. Intermittently he would chip away at each of his obstacles, always returning to the effort from a new angle. Significantly, David boasted he could handle any kind of problem, if he could deal with it in "small chunks." That was how David dealt with the constellation of feelings around each therapist—a little at a time, in ego-tolerating doses, rarely letting the emotional pressures become too much for him. Against group urging he would always set limits: "What's the big push? I don't have to settle everything I feel toward the group head at once! I'll get back to it. And if I don't do it here, I can always get my personal shrink to move it around." Where David felt constrained in one setting, he could feel free to delineate the individual components of his conflicts in the other.

To David the differing temperaments of the therapists were almost as important as their differing forms of treatment. The individual analyst's calm, objective attitude gave David room to reflect on his responses and impulses. He sensed that the therapist had feelings, wishes, and desires, yet did not act on them in their relationship. Thus the individual therapist set David a model of self-control.

David experienced the group leader somewhat differently. David saw the leader's energy, and his willingness to be involved, as an invitation to experiment with new ways of relating to others. The idea of taking an interpersonal gamble, of being open to new options, pointed the way to another mode of living. At this writing, David is becoming convinced that the group leader acts in the service of the group, working to remove the behavior-blocks that keep members at an emotional and communicative distance from each other.

Above all, David is beginning to rid himself of infantile ways of responding and behaving. He is reaching out in mature ways to his equals and authority figures.

# Chapter 10

# CONJOINT TREATMENT IN
# RETROSPECT

When practitioners use a particular therapeutic modality, they have particular goals for the patients that they are attempting to treat. Conjoint analysis, as the reader is now aware, has as its major concern the emotional maturation of the patient. Although we have mentioned the term, "maturation" several times throughout this book, a few comments are still in order.

By "maturation" we are not exclusively or even pre-dominantly concerned with certain kinds of behavior. The patient's behavior in and of itself does not help us understand what fantasies, defenses, or anxieties are at work. For example, an active sex life can be an expression of free flowing libido in a relatively mature person or it can be viewed as a compulsive defense in an anxious person.[5,6]

The reason we are offering the cautionary note about behavior is that the goal of "maturity" has too often been equated with helping the patient adapt to some arbitrary group norms instead of considering those forces that are operating within him, i.e., his subjective state, his wishes, fantasies, ego functions, etc. Indeed, some sociologists and social psychologists have been quite critical of psychoanalysts and psychotherapists for participating in a movement that they contend merely adjusts a person to a sick society.[1] Maturity, they have averred, assumes some acculturation in some group, and basically it is acculturation to the central mores of the widest society in which the person is an effective social unit. The sociologist Kingsley Davis in a statement on the psychotherapeutic movement has opined that the spirit governing modern psychotherapy is the Puritan Protestant ethic with its emphasis on rational thinking, utilitarian motives, individualism, and asceticism. Rather than enhancing individuals, psychoanalysis and psychotherapy, according to Davis, merely imposes a perverted middle-class value system on disturbed people.[1]

Hollingshead and Redlich have been able to show that our middle-class Protestant ethic and the institutional arrangements in our society tend to foster a situation in which individuals in lower socioeconomic classes suffer more emotional conflicts and receive much less humane treatment when they become patients of therapists.[3] Either they are treated like second-class citizens by therapists or the traditional middle-class values of therapists that are frequently imposed on them are dysfunctional for these patients.

No doubt all therapists are to some degree influenced by the prevailing norms in society. As our society has been emphasizing the futility of restraint and the importance of being stimulated, many modalities of treatment reflect this concern. Just as the good educator is supposed to "turn on" his students, and "provide good vibes," so too many therapists have been emphasizing the importance of "touching," "holding," and other forms of stimulation.[7] At a time when swinging, switching, and group sex are popular, some therapists have been promoting these behaviors as part of their therapy.[7]

Although our position regarding "maturity" does not emphasize the behavioral dimensions in the patient's life, they cannot be overlooked. Most patients who seek therapy or psychoanalysis present as their major complaint a dissatisfaction with certain behaviors in key relationships. Often the patient is dissatisfied with his behavior in marriage, on the job, with his children, or in other key relationships. Even when patients focus their discussions on how role partners are not gratifying them, implied is a question, "How can I behave differently so that I can get what I want?"

As the previous chapters of this book have revealed, our focus has been to sensitize the patient to his or her wishes, defenses, superego admonitions, etc., that propel the individual's behavior As immature cravings subside, neurotic defenses diminish. Sometimes there is a change of behavior, but of more importance, the patient looks at himself differently and his view of people alters. As he finds himself not chasing unrealistic fantasies as much, as he reduces his childish demands on people, as he sees reality more as it is and not as much as he wishes it to be, we have said that the patient is more "mature."

## WHAT IS MATURITY?

But, what is maturity? Dictionary definitions attempt to respond to the question by stating that to "mature" is "to ripen" or "to develop." However, the psychotherapist would want to ask and answer the further question, "Ripen into what?" or "Develop what capacities to do what?"

When the founder of psychoanalysis, Sigmund Freud, was asked these questions, he answered, "Lieben und arbiten"—"To love and to work." While loving and working usually are activities of the mature person, Freud did not expound too much on the nature of the love or the quality of the work to which he was alluding. Neither did he refer to the subjective state of the mature lover or mature worker.

Erik Erikson, in pondering Freud's terse definition of maturity, concluded that the prototype of mature love is the mutual orgasm, "a supreme experience of the mutual regulation of two beings . . . which breaks the point off the hostilities and potential rages caused by the oppositeness of male and female, of fact and fancy, of love and hate."[2] In relating to both "love and work" Erikson concluded that the mature person should be able to enjoy a "mutuality of orgasm with a loved partner of the other sex with whom one is able and willing to share a mutual trust and with whom one is able and willing to regulate the cycle of work, procreation, and recreation, so as to secure to the off-spring, too, a satisfactory development."[2]

The amplification of Freud's "love and work" pre-scription by Erikson can be taken as an ideal to achieve. No human being can love and work consistently without re-gressing from time to time. The mature person, we aver, is capable of accepting without too much guilt or shame his own limitations and imperfections. Furthermore, he should be able not only to renounce most of his infantile, omnipo-tent wishes, but he should be able to genuinely accept the limitations and imperfections in others. The mature person does not have strong residues of anger and hatred towards his parents and significant others for not being able to be perfect parents. He can forgive others in the present and past for not meeting his wishes the way they should have, or the way he would have liked them to have done so.[5]

While the mature person should be able to give and take love, empathize with his or her partner's needs and enjoy the partner's doing likewise, he or she is able to have enough of a self-image and sufficient autonomy that the lack of love or lack of validation of his own ego does not humiliate or destroy him. The mature person has a sense of his own completeness and integrity so that he can like himself even when others do not view him so positively. He has achieved enough separateness from past introjects so that he can agree with the playwright Ibsen, who wrote, "The strongest man is he who stands alone."

For the maturer person, love and work do not have too much of a compulsive quality. He or she can enjoyably and spontaneously participate in both without needing either for purposes of proving himself to himself.

Although within our notion of maturity are some behavioral referents, we are most concerned with the patient's psychic structure. In our definition of maturity, the patient has developed a "strong ego." He can, for example, tolerate frustration and forego certain gratifications when they are not attainable, or in the best interest of himself or others. He can judge reality as it is and not as he wishes it to be. Decision making and problem solving is accepted as a fact of life because he has tamed omnipotent wishes in himself and does not fantasize others as omnipotent parents. The mature person has been able to renounce some of his narcissism and derive satisfaction from giving to, identifying, and empathizing with others.

Although the mature person can judge and accept reality as it is, he can concomitantly enjoy pleasure. He can enjoy his or her sexual role, take initiative as a man or woman with his partner and without thinking or wishing that he or she is supplanting somebody else. His superego is not harsh and because he accepts life as it is, he does not have to be punished for aggressive thoughts or actions.

## DIAGNOSING IMMATURITIES

We have commented at some length on our notions of "maturity" because we have taken the position throughout this book that essentially therapy is designed to help the patient overcome the immature dimensions of his psychic structure. As our case illustrations have demonstrated, in conjoint analyses childish cravings, archaic defenses, and inappropriate superego voices were constantly addressed in the individual and group treatments. It is our conviction that when an individual is experiencing psychosocial difficulties and expresses them through neurotic symptomology, pathological character traits, or psychoses, his psychosocial processes have either *regressed* to or are *fixated* at a childhood level of development. Either the individual has experienced severe amounts of anxiety which make his usual level of functioning too difficult and consequently he returns to where life was easier (regression), or else the patient has never really grown up at all (fixation). In either case, we conclude, the individual has not been able, or is currently not able, to master a maturational task.[5]

As Erikson[2] and others[5,6] have demonstrated, every child in the process of growing up has a maturational timetable. To grow and develop healthfully requires certain experiences: the nourishment and comfort in the womb, the vigilance and tenderness of a loving and nurturing mother after birth, nonabruptive and planned weaning, toilet-training that is neither too indulgent or restrictive so that autonomy and independence will be stimulated, sexual information that is pallative but not excessive, to name but just a few experiences necessary for successful maturation.[5,6]

Because the growing child has different psychosocial needs at different levels of maturation, he or she needs an environment that will offer age-appropriate experiences, for example, he needs to be held frequently and fed on demand when he is a suckling infant. If the child's environment meets his maturational needs appropriately, that is, gives him what he needs when he needs it, relative maturity and mental health will be assured. However, if the growing youngster is insufficiently gratified, frustrated excessively, or is indulged, he will be constantly seeking to gratify immature cravings. For example, alcoholism exists in both patients who have been poorly nourished emotionally and physically and in individuals who have been inappropriately weaned.[5]

For a developmental or maturational task to be mastered, the child, therefore, must experience appropriate doses of gratification and frustration. As we have suggested above, at birth and for the next several months, the child should experience a tender, loving, nurturing relationship with his mother. If this is not forthcoming, depression, self-hate, psychic disorganization, and possibly psychosis can develop. On the other hand, if the child is not appropriately weaned from the breast or bottle, if the mother-child symbiosis is not loosened, if the child is not assisted enough to take on some independent functioning and autonomy, then he may very well emerge into an overdemanding, highly dependent, hungry individual who imposes severe burdens on others.[5,6]

We have taken the position throughout this volume that most, if not all, individuals who seek psychotherapy or psychoanalysis are either fixated at or have regressed to an earlier level of maturational development. Their past environments and relationships with significant others and/or their current environments and current relationships have not or are not providing them with the appropriate experiences of frustration and/or gratification to help them cope with intra- and interpersonal tasks of life. The patient either wants what is unreasonable and unattainable or is too frightened to seek out what is realistically attainable and potentially satisfying.

Because our orientation states that the patient has certain maturational needs unfulfilled, he emerges in the therapeutic encounter as a child who needs experiences that will help him master maturational tasks. In diagnosing the patient's ego functions, we ask in every case: "Where is the patient hung up? Has he been improperly nurtured during the first year of life either by inconsistent, frustrated, or excessive feeding? Have tiolet training and other tasks been imposed prematurely or abruptly?" Or perhaps limit-setting was not done enough? Has the patient been sufficiently acculturated to his or her sexual role? Was there too much seduction or perhaps insufficient admiration of him or her as a maturing sexual boy or girl? How were inevitable separations such as going to school experienced by the patient? Were they premature? Were they handled ambivalently?

## TREATMENT IN RETROSPECT

We have conceptualized the roles of the therapist or psychoanalyst as one who is, in effect, a maturational agent. The therapist, like the mature and loving parent, should provide in the treatment, appropriate maturational experiences of frustration and gratification depending on where his patient is psychosocially. Correct diagnosis contains within it the maturational task or tasks that the patient cannot cope with by himself or herself. For example, if the maturational task requires feeding, then the therapist must offer verbal forms of feeding, for example, praise, overt interest, verbal exchange, etc. If the patient is depressed, as another example, the maturational need for the patient is, in all likelihood, to discharge verbal agression at the therapist. If the patient is seeking indulgences, the role of the therapist or analyst is to explore and question the patient's requests without gratifying them.[5]

The therapist, utilizing the paradigm of the mature parent, should ask, "Does my child need limits and structure, or silence and distance, or stimulation, withdrawal, sex information or just what?" As the maturing child needs different responses from key maturational agents at different stages of his development, so, too, the patient at one stage of treatment may need praise and support and, at another, silence and nonresponsiveness. The mature therapist offers his patient what the latter needs, uncontaminated by the therapist's wishes or unfulfilled fantasies.[5]

In our view the therapist must attempt at all times to assess where his symbolic child is maturationally and therefore how he is experienced by the patient. The transference relationship of the patient is, in effect, the barometer we can utilize to inform us where the patient is in his therapeutic maturation. Are we experienced as the depriving mother who should feed? Or, are we experienced as the depriving mother who should not feed because we will encourage further regression? Are we the overly seductive mother or father, as the patient experiences us in the transference, or the mother or father who is not sufficiently responsive? In answering these questions we can determine and then offer what the patient needs: warmth and verbal feeding or cool detachment and silence, intelligent guidance or refusal to offer advice, permissiveness or structure, discipline and restraint, or praise or criticism.

## THE CONTRIBUTION OF CONJOINT ANALYSIS

Although many therapists and analysts do subscribe to the aforementioned notions on treatment, we feel that the organization of therapy in conjoint analysis offers several additional advantages. Because the human organism has to cope from birth to death with two crucial tasks, namely interacting and transacting with himself and, in addition, coping, interacting, and transacting with others, the opportunities available in conjoint analysis parallel these two maturational tasks.

As was noted in the vignettes presented, when patients are offered the opportunity of studying their fantasies, dreams, fears, wishes, and transference reactions in their individual treatment, they can experiment in the group setting with their new insights and learn how their strengths, limitations, anxieties, and resistances are perceived and received by others. Furthermore, as the patient is able in the group setting to learn more about some of his or her habitual ways of coping with interpersonal relationships and interpersonal conflicts, particularly the immature wishes and stresses that are involved in his interpersonal encounters, the patient can then proceed to examine more carefully in individual treatment some of the genetic forces and other factors that contribute to his less mature ego functioning.

We have also learned from our experience in conjoint analysis that the availability of two therapists has some distinct advantages. Not only do two therapists activate in dynamic form how the patient experiences his two parents within a triangle, but the wishes that many patients have for an omnipotent parent are sharply reduced. When the patient observes different therapeutic styles and different therapeutic personalities at work, he is less apt to feel that his childish fantasies for the perfect parent can be realized. Rather, he begins to realize fairly early in treatment that bliss is momentary and the Garden of Eden is not attainable.

Conjoint analysis, based on a psychosocial orientation to the human organism that never divorces the individual's psychic functioning from his interpersonal processes is one therapy that appears to reduce neurotic suffering and seems to enhance self-esteem, reality testing, and other functions of the ego.

# REFERENCES

## CHAPTER 1: TOWARDS A PSYCHOSOCIAL VIEW OF THE HUMAN BEING: RELEVANT THEORY

1. Adler, A. *Problems of neuroses.* New York: Harper Torchbooks, 1964.
2. Alexander, F. & French, T. *Psychoanalytic therapy.* New York: Ronald Press, 1946.
3. Brenner, C. *An elementary textbook of psychoanalysis.* Doubleday, Garden City, N.Y.: 1955.
4. Erikson, E. H. *Childhood and society.* New York: W. W. Norton, 1963.
5. Erikson, E. H. Identity and the life cycle. *Psychological Issues,* Monograph I. New York: International Universities Press, 1959.
6. Erikson, E. H. *Insight and responsibility.* New York: W. W. Norton, 1964.
7. Ferenczi, S. & Rank, O. *The development of psychoanalysis.* New York: Nervous and Mental Disease Publishing Co., 1925.
8. Ferenczi, S. *Further contributions to the theory and technique of psychoanalysis.* London: Hogarth Press, 1926.
9. Fine, R. Psychoanalysis. In R. Corsini (Ed.), *Current psychotherapies.* Itasca, Ill: F. E. Peacock Publishers, 1973.
10. Fine, R. *Freud: a critical re-evaluation of his theories.* New York: David McKay, 1962.

11. Freud, A. *The ego and the mechanisms of defense.* London: Hogarth Press, 1928.

12. Freud, S. *The standard edition of the complete psychological works of Sigmund Freud.* London: Hogarth Press, 1953–1964. 24 vols.

13. Hartmann, H. *Essays on ego psychology: selected problems in psychoanalytic theory.* New York: International Universities Press, 1964.

14. Hartmann, H. *Ego psychology and the problem of adaptation.* New York: International Universities Press, 1958.

15. Hartmann, H. Comments on the psychoanalytic theory of the ego. In *The psychoanalytic study of the child.* (Vol. 5) ed. A. Freud. New York: International Universities Press, 1950.

16. Moreno, J. *Psychodrama.* (Vol. 2) New York: Beacon House, 1959.

17. Mullan, H. & Sanguiliano, I. Existential matrix of psychotherapy. *Psychoanalytic Review,* 1960, **47**(4), 87–99.

18. Munroe, R. *Schools of psychoanalytic thought.* New York: Henry Holt, 1955.

19. Nelson, M., Nelson, B., Sherman, M., & Strean, H. *Roles and paradigms in psychotherapy.* New York: Grune & Stratton, 1968.

20. Rappaport, D. The structure of psychoanalytic theory: a systematizing attempt. In S. Koch (Ed.) *Psychology: a study of a science.* (Vol. 3) New York: McGraw-Hill, 1951.

21. Spotnitz, H. *Modern psychoanalysis of the schizophrenic patient.* New York: Grune & Stratton, 1967.

22. Strean, H. *The social worker as psychotherapist.* Metuchen, N. J.: Scarecrow Press, 1974.

23. Strean, H. *The experience of psychotherapy.* Metuchen, N. J.: Scarecrow Press, 1973.

24. Sullivan, H. S. Conceptions of modern psychiatry. In *Psychiatry.* (Vol. 3) p. 1–117, 1940.

25. Wood, K. The contribution of psychoanalysis and ego psychology to social casework. In H. Strean (Ed.), *Social Casework: Theories in Action.* Metuchen, N. J.: Scarecrow Press, 1972.

26. Wyss, D. *Psychoanalytic schools.* New York: Jason Aronson Press, 1973.

## CHAPTER 2: THE THERAPEUTIC RATIONALE FOR CONJOINT TREATMENT

1. Bibring-Lehner, G. Contribution of the subject of transference resistance. *International Journal of Psychoanalysis,* 1936, **17**, 181–189.

2. Fine, R. *The healing of the mind.* New York: David Mackay, 1971.
3. Freud, S. *A general introduction to psychoanalysis.* Garden City, N.Y.: Garden City Publishers, 1943.
4. Freud, S. Remembering, repeating, and working through. *Collected Papers.* London: Hogarth Press, 1949, **2**, 366–376.
5. Lipschutz, I. Group psychotherapy as an auxiliary aid in psychoanalysis. *International Journal of Group Psychotherapy,* 1952, **2**, 316–323.
6. Nelson, M., Nelson, B., Sherman, M., & Strean, H. *Roles and paradigms in psychotherapy.* New York: Grune & Stratton, 1968.
7. Ormont, L. The resolution of resistances by conjoint psychoanalysis. *The Psychoanalytic Review,* 1964, **51**, 89–101.
8. Ormont, L. (with Hunt, M., Corman, R.) *The Talking Cure.* New York: Harper, 1964.
9. Ormont, L. The use of the objective countertransference to resolve group resistances. *The Group Process,* 1970–71, **3**, 95–111.
10. Rickman, J. *Selected contribution to psycho-analysis.* London: Hogarth Press, 1957.
11. Roscow, M. & Kaplan, L. Integrated individual and group therapy. *International Journal of Group Psychotherapy,* 1954, **4**, 381–392.
12. Spotnitz, H. *The modern psychoanalysis of the schizophrenic patient.* New York: Grune & Stratton, 1969.
13. Strean, H. *The experience of psychotherapy.* Metuchen, N.J.: Scarecrow Press, 1973.

## CHAPTER 3: LIMITATIONS AND CONTRAINDICATIONS OF CONJOINT TREATMENT

1. Bach, G. R. *Intensive group psychotherapy.* New York: Ronald Press, 1954.
2. Bibring-Lehner, G. Contribution of the subject of transference resistance. *International Journal of Psychoanalysis,* 1936, **17**, 181–189.
3. Clevans, E. The depressive reaction. *Modern Psychoanalysis,* 1976, **1**, 139–148.
4. Greenacre, P. *Emotional growth.* New York: International Universities Press, 1971, pp. 651–670.
5. Roscow, M. & Kaplan, L. Integrated individual and group therapy. *International Journal of Group Psychotherapy,* 1954, **4**, 381–392.
6. Rosenbaum, M. The psychoanalytic group: formation and beginnings. *Group Process,* 1976, **7**, 9–35.

7. Schwartz, E. & Wolf, A. *Psychoanalysis in groups.* New York: Grune & Stratton, 1962.
8. Slavson, H. *Analytic group psychotherapy.* New York: Columbia University Press, 1950.
9. Spotnitz, H. & Meadow, P. *Treatment of the narcissistic neuroses.* New York: Manhattan Center for Modern Psychoanalysis, 1976.

## CHAPTER 4: THE PATIENT IN INDIVIDUAL TREATMENT

1. Erikson, E. *Childhood and society.* New York: Norton, 1950.
2. Fine, R. *The healing of the mind.* New York: David McKay, 1971.
3. Fine, R. Psychoanalysis. In R. Corsini (Ed.), *Current psychotherapies.* Ithasca, Ill.: Peacock Publishers, 1973.
4. Freud, S. Remembering, repeating, and working through (1914). *Standard Edition.* (Vol. 14) London: Hogarth Press, 1966.
5. Greenson, R. *The technique and practice of psychoanalysis.* New York: International Universities Press, 1967.
6. Harley, M. *The analyst and the adolescent at work.* New York: Quadrangle, 1974.
7. Hartmann, H. *Essays on ego psychology.* New York: International Universities Press, 1958
8. Nelson, M., Nelson, B., Sherman, M., & Strean, H. *Roles and paradigms in psychotherapy.* New York: Grune & Stratton, 1968.
9. Reich, A. *Psychoanalytic contributions.* New York: International Universities Press, 1963.
10. Spotnitz, H. *Modern psychoanalysis of the schizophrenic patient.* New York: Grune & Stratton, 1967.
11. Strean, H. *The experience of psychotherapy.* Metuchen, N.J.: Scarecrow Press, 1972.
12. Zetzel, E. Defense mechanisms and psychoanalytic technique. *Journal of the American Psychoanalytic Association,* 1955, **2,** 318–326.

## CHAPTER 5: THE PATIENT IN GROUP TREATMENT

1. Altman, L. L., *The dream in psychoanalysis.* New York: International Universities Press, 1969.
2. Bion, W. R. *Experience in groups.* New York: Basic Books, 1959.
3. Ezriel, H. A psychoanalytic approach to group treatment. *British Journal of Medical Psychology,* 1952, **23,** 119–126.
4. Kadis, A. L. Early childhood recollections as aids in group psychotherapy. *Journal of Individual Psychology,* 1957, **13,** 182–187.

5.  Ormont, L. R. Establishing the analytic contract in a newly formed therapeutic group. *British Journal of Medical Psychology,* 1962, **35,** 333–337.
6.  Ormont, L. R. Acting in and the therapeutic contract in group psychoanalysis. *International Journal of Group Therapy,* 1969, **11,** 420–432.
7.  Ormont, L. R. Group resistance and the therapeutic contract, *International Journal of Group Psychotherapy,* 1968, **18,** 147–154.
8.  Spotnitz, H. *The couch and the circle.* New York: Alfred A. Knopf, 1961.

## CHAPTER 6: MAJOR GROUP RESISTANCES

1.  Ormont, L. R. The use of the objective countertransference to resolve group resistances. *Group Process,* 1970–71, **2,** 95–111.
2.  Rosenthal, L. Resolution of group destructive resistance in modern group analysis. *Modern Psychoanalysis,* 1976, **1,** 243–256.
3.  Spotnitz, H. The toxoid responses. *Psychoanalytic Review,* 1963, **50,** 612–624.
4.  Wolf, A. & Schwartz, E. *Psychoanalysis in groups.* New York: Grune & Stratton, 1962.

## CHAPTER 7: PREPARING THE GROUP FOR THE INDIVIDUAL

1.  Kaplan, S. R. & Roman, M. Characteristic responses in adult therapy to the introduction of new members: a reflection of group processes. *International Journal of Group Psychotherapy,* 1961, **11,** 372–381.
2.  Ormont, L. R. The preparation of patients for group psychoanalysis. *American Journal of Psychotherapy,* 1957, **11,** 841–848.
3.  Strean, H. S. *New approaches in child guidance.* Metuchen, N. J.: Scarecrow Press, 1970.

## CHAPTER 10: CONJOINT TREATMENT IN RETROSPECT

1.  Davis, K. Mental hygiene and the class structure. In H. Stein & R. Cloward (Eds.), *Social perspectives on behavior.* New York: Free Press, 1958.

2. Erikson, E. *Childhood and society.* New York: W. W. Norton, 1950.
3. Hollingshead, A. B. & Redlich, F. C. Social stratification and psychiatric disorders. In H. Stein & R. Cloward (Eds.), *Social perspectives on behavior.* New York: Free Press, 1958.
4. Riesmann, F., Cohen, J., & Pearl, A. *Mental health of the poor.* New York: Free Press, 1964.
5. Strean, H. *The experience of psychotherapy.* Metuchen, N. J.: Scarecrow Press, 1973.
6. Strean, H. *The social worker as psychotherapist.* Metuchen, N. J.: Scarecrow Press, 1974.
7. Strean, H. Social change and the proliferation of regressive therapies. *The Psychoanalytic Review,* in *Crucial Issues in Psychotherapy,* ed. H. Strean, Scarecrow Press, Metuchen, N. J.: 1976.

# INDEX

227